INVESTSIGHTS
SERIES

Investment Banking
Insider's Guide:

How to Get Into Wall Street from the
Outside and Survive When You're In

First Edition, Copyright © 2006 by John Wise

First printed by Lulu Publishing (www.lulu.com).

ISBN: 978-1-4303-0052-6

I. Introduction

So you want to be an investment banker, or at least considering it. The prestige, the money, the excitement, or maybe just the doors it will open if you start out in investment banking. Whatever your reasons, the more you learn about it, the better off you will be in making your decision.

Okay, another "insiders" guide, so what? Why should I read this, you might ask yourself. First of all, let me give you a couple disclaimers:

1. This is not going to be the most comprehensive guide out there, nor is it intended to be.

2. Secondly, no matter how wonderfully comprehensive or wonderful this guide may be, if you don't follow the advice, you can't write me about how terrible the guide was.

3. Thirdly, some people reading this may disagree with some of my comments or even be angered that I've put out such a guide because it takes away from their competitive advantage. That's ok, I'm not writing to please everyone, but to help those who need it and want the help. The comments are solely my opinion.

4. Lastly, if in fact you used the guide, and found the information to be useless, then please send me an email (johnwise@investsights.com) on what I can do to improve it; this will benefit other readers as well.

I am always open to constructive criticism, so don't be shy in letting me know your thoughts. Feedback is always appreciated, both positive and constructive.

Now that the disclaimers are out of the way, let's get to some other points:

- Who is the guy writing this and why would you want to listen to him?

- Who should read this?

- Why should you read this instead of (or in addition to) some other guides?

Who is the author?

Let me start by introducing myself. This book is written under a pen name John Wise because I don't want some angry Human Resources (HR) people coming after me for disclosing some of the inside scoop. I was an immigrant from Southeast Asia and grew up in a small town in Wisconsin. I graduated from Yale in 1997 with an Economics degree and have been on Wall Street for over eight years, excluding my summer internships. My initial introduction to investment banking came about as a summer intern in the Sponsors for Educational Opportunity (SEO) Career Program (I'll describe this program later on) for two consecutive summers where I had direct exposure to the major Wall Street firms. Prior to that, I had no clue what investment banking was and actually started college as a pre-med expecting to go into genetics engineering or some medical-related field after graduation.

Right out of college, I joined J.P. Morgan & Company (now called JP Morgan Chase) in the Analyst Training Program in Investment Banking, starting out by working on acquisition financing and commercial lending transactions in the Credit Department. Then I transferred to the Technology, Media & Telecom Mergers & Acquisitions Group during the boom years of the technology bubble in 1999. I was a direct promote from an Analyst to an Associate without pursuing an MBA degree. After J.P. Morgan, I was one of the first guys hired by Barclays Capital to help build up the Corporate Finance Advisory Group from scratch. I left Barclays at the beginning of 2003 and joined a well-known media & telecom investment banking boutique called Daniels & Associates. Most recently, I was at Citigroup until February of 2006, and now pursuing more entrepreneurial endeavors, while writing this guide.

So why am I telling you all this about my background? Simply to confirm that I've been there, I was an outsider with no connections who became an insider and this guide provides a summary of my experiences on how you can get there too, how to survive while you're there, and ways to succeed when you've made it in. Of course, when I say "my experience," that's not entirely correct because this guide essentially is a compilation of my personal experience and the lessons I've learned from others who have mentored me and those I've mentored along the way. It would be presumptuous of me to claim that I am the most qualified person to provide you with the perfect solution to getting into Wall Street. Obviously there is no perfect approach that guarantees you entrance to Wall Street, and each individual reading this will have his or her own unique circumstances, but hopefully, some of the advice and points that I've made in this guide will prove useful to the majority of people thinking about entering Wall Street as an investment banker.

Who should read this?

Perhaps it's easier if I start by saying who this isn't for. If you're looking for a reference guide that tells you about stocks and bonds and the history of Wall Street, this is not it. There are plenty of good comprehensive guides out there that serve those purposes. Instead, this pragmatic guide is a high level overview that should get you through the interview process (yes, I've done lots of interviews from both an interviewer as well as interviewee perspective), as well as to do well as an analyst. An undergraduate college student thinking of getting into Wall Street should definitely read this. If you're an MBA student who didn't have any experience prior to business school and want to get into Wall Street, this could be helpful even though it's targeted to undergraduates. I wrote this guide because my younger sister was starting her summer internship at a Wall Street firm and had absolutely no idea what the difference between stocks and bonds are, let alone what investment banking is all about, so I had to sit down and walk her through it. There are other guides out there, many were written after I had already entered Wall Street, and still seem to miss certain points that I think are vital.

Why should you read this instead of, or in addition to, other guides?

I didn't grow up with a silver spoon; in fact my parents were on welfare when I was younger, so my upbringing was humble to say the least. I had no insider connections to get me access to the right people to talk to, and as we all know, connections are crucial, especially on Wall Street. My ability to get to where I am today is a function of hard work, significant luck and initiative. This guide is written from the perspective of what I wish I had known when I first thought about getting an investment banking job.   I will tell you things which some recruiters and analysts, and even your fellow classmates who are more connected than you are, may not want you to know, and while some will disagree with my viewpoints, please bear in mind that each individual's experience will be unique.   The intent of this guide is to put you on par with people who already have connections. The dollars you spent to buy this guide will prove the best return on investment in your future if you leverage the information for the investment banking interviews, whether it's for a summer internship, or for a full time position. Because the purpose of this guide is intended to be a high level exposure for the inexperienced and non-connected, I've included a list of reading materials at the end that I found helpful for those interested in more depth.   I sincerely hope that the information I provide in this guide will contribute to your future success.

II. Overview of Investment Banking – The Basics

This chapter is dedicated to people who have never had an internship in investment banking before, or those who have had internships in investment banking, but were too focused on impressing their bosses to step back and really understand what banking is all about. Again, I will reiterate that this is not meant to be a comprehensive guide, but meant to give you enough information to understand at a high level and be able to get past all the interviews.

What is investment banking?

Simply and generally put, investment banking is the matching of those who need money with those who have money. This is as basic as you can get when defining what people refer to as "investment banking." Sometimes investment banking is synonymous with Wall Street. Others would argue that investment banking should only refer more specifically to corporate finance or M&A. Now exactly what does that mean?

An investment banker is essentially an intermediary. Imagine if you have a great idea and wanted to start a business with it, but you don't have the money. You don't come from a wealthy family and you don't have rich relatives, but you're too young to get a loan from a bank. So where can you get the money to start your business? Well you're in luck, you have a friend who happens to know a lot of rich people and he offers to help you out by introducing you to those rich people to pitch your idea...for a fee. Your friend essentially works as an investment banker in that case by getting you connected to potential financiers for your idea. Obviously that's a very simplistic way of thinking about investment banking, but the concept applies: investment bankers are ultimately intermediaries. If you knew the rich people yourself, you wouldn't need your friend and could avoid paying the introduction fees. The same applies to companies that need financing, they wouldn't hire investment bankers if they could find the money themselves.

Now that you understand the concept, it's important to understand the key divisions of investment banking and how they are integrated. The following diagram shows the traditional segments of most investment banks.

Major Investment Banking Divisions

Most major investment banks are very diversified with other businesses (for example, investment management, private banking, prime brokerage, etc.) that are beyond the scope of the discussion of this guide.

Before I delve into the key divisions, let me first explain the "Chinese Wall", so named after the Great Wall of China given its intended obstruction to separate the inside from the outside. By "inside," this refers to information that is confidential. When you hear about insider trading, it's the illegal practice where an individual executes a transaction using privately held confidential information that you would not be able to find in the public realm. For example, if the CEO of a publicly traded company knows that his firm is about to report a major contract that will significantly improve the company's financial performance, he can buy the stock before the announcement and expect with relative certainty the stock price to go up significantly following the announcement, thus making a guaranteed riskless profit from the trade. Since others outside the management team or outside of the firm are not aware of this inside information, it is illegal for the CEO to make such a trade.

From the previous diagram, you can see which departments in general have access to confidential information versus publicly reported information about a company. When a publicly listed client hires an investment banker to buy another company, usually the investment banker in the Mergers & Acquisitions department will be provided with confidential information about the client company and is strictly prohibited from any personal financial dealing that uses such information...i.e., he can't go out and start trading the client's stock in his personal brokerage account.

Notice in the diagram that the Capital Markets division sits on top of the Chinese wall. The explanation for this will be clear in the description of the department's role, which I will get to shortly.

Mergers & Acquisitions (M&A)

Mergers and acquisitions or "M&A" is probably the most well-known area within investment banking. The department is the execution group for transactions that you usually see reported in the Wall Street Journal and the glamorized aspect of Wall Street that you see in movies. M&A is a product group, meaning if you work in that group, you'll probably be executing transactions across several industries. Of course, certain industries are a bit more technical, so they will likely have M&A specialists concentrating on those specific areas; it's just too difficult for someone to try and learn the jargon and technical aspects of those industries over a short period of time. Examples include telecom and biotech, both require deep industry knowledge that are better suited to specialists rather than generalists. Some firms integrate the M&A division with their industry groups rather than having a separate M&A division, so it's important to understand how the firms are structured. Unfortunately, investment banks have gone through various cycles in which they integrate, then separate, then go through the cycle again as they endure periods of boom and bust: during boom periods M&A usually is separated since there are plenty of transactions to justify an independent group, but when deals dry up and headcount becomes redundant, the groups usually get merged into their respective industry focus.

Many who want to go into investment banking want to get into M&A, but before you jump onto that band wagon, I'll give you the good, the bad and the ugly aspects.   M&A is probably the hardest group to get into and usually gets to pick the cream of the crop out of the analyst pool at most investment banks. But there is also a huge trade-off. While it may garner the prestige and excitement, it also represents one of the hardest working divisions (not that other areas of investment banking are a breeze), with 100+ hour work weeks not being uncommon for new hires during the first year. The "asshole factor" and "big egos" are also pretty high in M&A relative to other areas of investment banking, it just seems to go with the stereotype.

If you can put up with those factors and the long hours, then the upside is pretty high. Since M&A tends to hone analytical and modeling skills, most analysts that have completed two years in M&A will have a variety of options available outside of banking. The most likely track seems to be private equity, although now given the popularity of hedge funds over the past couple years, that's another area that has become a natural switch after an analyst program.

Corporate Finance

Corporate finance is a broad term that may mean slightly different things to different people.   Essentially, it is how companies finance themselves. While capital markets may be lumped into the corporate finance bucket, I've chosen to separate the two since the roles and responsibilities seem to be slightly different in terms of the experience for the analyst/associate, although both are not exclusive from one another and often are working in conjunction with one another on a large transaction. There are two main areas of corporate finance as I've defined it: Credit and Private Placement

- **Credit** – This is the division where bank facilities are originated and applies to investment grade companies, meaning companies that are of good credit quality (typically the case for large Fortune 500 industrial conglomerates). Commercial loans (just another name for bank facilities) are essentially like any other personal loans except much bigger, and usually due to their size, syndicated (meaning there are more than one lender). Imagine if you were looking to get a $100 loan from someone. You probably don't need to borrow it from more than one person. But if you were going to borrow $5000, most likely you're going to borrow it from a number of people, each lending you, say $500 each. Similarly, when a large corporation wants to borrow say $1 billion+, it will hire a bank to raise that money. The investment banker in the Credit department will help the client raise the money by forming a syndicate of lenders, each agreeing to lend a chunk of the money. The reasons for why a syndicate is formed rather than having the main bank provide the whole loan are fairly straightforward:

  ✓ Bank facilities are very low margin businesses, so banks usually don't like to provide them; they do so because their clients need the loans and therefore pressure the banks to provide them before giving the lending banks some other business (such as an M&A advisory assignment or IPO) to make up for the low returns on the loans.

    ✓ Loans are risky, so by having a syndicate, all the lenders share the risk proportionately to the amount they lent.

    ✓ By putting less money into one client, there's more capital that can be deployed to other clients, and thus, allow the bank to get other businesses from other clients.

By nature of the lending business, your concern as a credit analyst is downside risk. You don't get much upside (your upside is the fee that you charge for helping to syndicate the loan and the interest that is charged on the loan), but your downside is much greater...the total amount of the loan you just agreed to lend! Hence, the mentality of most credit bankers tends to be much more conservative. Usually when you see two financial models created, one by a banker in credit and one by a banker in M&A, the projections tend to be much more optimistic from the M&A side. While most bankers from the advisory side (M&A or industry groups) tend to look down at the credit department, the value of the training in credit is often under appreciated. Having had experience in both areas, I would say that while the skills and training in both areas are highly similar, the personalities of bankers in those divisions tend to be almost complete opposites. Credit/commercial bankers tend to be much more low-key and conservative when analyzing a company...a common characterization would be that they tend to be "nicer" personalities. Furthermore, generally speaking, while investment bankers typically transition to business development roles or CFO positions, credit bankers transition to treasurer roles at corporations. Obviously there will always be exceptions to the rule, but those are common tracks.

- **Private Placement** – This division refers to the area where a company does not have access to the public markets and needs financings. As a company that is not rated (say by a major rating agency such as Moody's and Standard & Poor's), they are not able to raise money by issuing public bonds. The company is also usually not publicly listed (they don't have stock that is traded on a stock exchange), so they can't just issue stock to raise money in the equity market. So they turn to the investment bankers in the private placement division who can help them sell their securities to investors by privately placing those securities with investors directly. Without going into the technical aspects of why or how this is done, the concept is simply that a company wants to raise money in the private markets, these are the bankers who will know which investors to contact that may be interested in providing the money to them. Again, the banker serves as an intermediary and the potential sources of financing could be in the form of debt or equity. Generally speaking, the securities that are sold to ("placed" with) investors are not publicly listed and do not trade (and therefore are not registered with the Securities and Exchange Commission that regulates all public securities), hence the term "private."

Sales & Trading (S&T)

The sales and trading division is the department responsible for the trading of securities, whether they be stocks, bonds, currencies, options or even loans after the securities have been underwritten and issued. Ultimately, this is the division that makes the market for a specific security. The role of the sales folks is to try and get institutional investors (companies like Fidelity, Putnam, and other asset management firms) to buy a specific security. Traders on the other hand are responsible for executing trades for the banks clients, and they try to make a profit by capturing any price discrepancies in the market for the security that they're responsible for. Traders can be located in front of a computer terminal executing orders directly, or be located on an exchange floor such as the New York Stock Exchange. Trades can only be based on publicly available information, hence the S&T division is outside the Chinese wall.

Unlike M&A or corporate finance where the hours are longer and the stress more stretched out, the S&T division endures high stress over a shorter period of time. If you're not a morning person, sales and trading may not be the ideal choice. The sales & trading floor is usually full of high intensity and "in-your-face" personalities. Swearing is not uncommon, if not routine. The general stereotypes for people going into sales & trading are jocks, fraternity types, and nerdy quantitative types. Traditionally, it's a high testosterone environment, although there is increasingly more women penetrating and succeeding on the trading floor.

An advantage of analysts going into sales & trading is that usually there is no expectation or pressure for them to go on to business school. Analysts in other areas are usually hired for a two-year program, those that excel are offered a third year opportunity and may be considered for promotions to associates without pursuing an MBA (usually 20-30% of the class). Should the individual decide to leave sales & trading, the most likely transition would be to a hedge fund or other asset management firm.

Research

The research division of an investment bank publishes the research reports that make recommendations to institutional investors regarding a particular stock (or bond in the case of fixed income research), usually have ratings such as "Buy", "Sell", "Hold" among other gradations. In addition, the reports published are also widely used by bankers in corporate finance and M&A to build the financial models. Research analysts typically are considered experts in the sectors that they cover, so it makes sense that their projections and financial models serve as the basis for many valuation models created by the corporate finance and M&A bankers. Even though they sit outside the Chinese wall, they are brought inside the wall for initial public offerings, which simply means that they will be utilized by the corporate finance bankers to go on presentations helping to pitch the client's stock on a road show to meet with various institutional investors; when that happens, that research analyst will no longer be allowed to publish research until after the transaction has been completed.

While it does not have the glamour that it once held, the role of research continues to be an essential aspect of investment banking. In the past, the research department has been instrumental for transaction pitches as the corporate finance departments relied on strong recommendations from the research analysts to tout an idea. A function of how research departments were compensated had been driven by how many deals they help the corporate finance or M&A departments obtain. Recent regulations prohibit such interaction and now the main role of research is to help generate commissions for the bank from institutional investors that route their trades to the firm's trading floor. Theoretically, this results in research reports that are less biased on their recommendations given the disconnection with corporate finance or M&A.

Generally speaking, most analysts that go into research tend to be a bit more academic; they are usually referred to as "research associates" when they first start out, but for the sake of simplicity and avoiding confusion, I'll keep the term analysts. There are usually fewer positions in research and most analysts have done a year in corporate finance or M&A prior to joining those positions as a lifestyle change, since the hours are usually better (more specifically, weekends are usually free except for earnings season which happens once every quarter or major transaction events of the companies being covered). The rationale for this can be understood by the responsibilities. Research does not typically offer a training program, although some banks have new analysts go through the summer training along with corporate finance or M&A analysts. Given the team is typically very small, perhaps there will be one or two other junior members on the team supporting one senior research analyst covering a particular sector, you really will not get a lot of lateral support outside that team. The modeling and analytical skills required in research are similar to that from corporate finance and M&A, so the transition is typically quite simple.

I should note that the term "research analyst" should not be confused with an analyst coming into an investment banking program. A senior research analyst can have the title of Managing Director or Vice President, and the junior members supporting them are typically referred to as research associates; the senior research analyst is essentially the firm's resident expert on a particular sector. The most well-known ones (and justifiably best paid ones) are ranked in the top 3 by Institutional Investors (often simply referred to as "II-ranked") for the sectors they cover. Working for someone II-ranked significantly improves the junior members' options as they seek to become senior research analysts themselves.

As a junior team member, the role is to support the senior research analysts. Responsibilities will vary depending on experience and ability. Among some of the key roles, a junior member is responsible for building the financial models on the specific companies covered, interacting with traders and the sales team, as well as answering questions fielded by investors' calls, and most importantly, writing the research reports. Typically you will be gathering data to support a particular thesis/theme. Contrary to popular belief, most senior research analysts, particularly the II-ranked ones, spend most of their time talking to investors rather than writing the research reports. Their value for the firm is to be the "go to" person that institutional investors want to call when they have questions about a particular sector/company that are covered by that research analyst; obviously the more relationships they have with key investors, the more likely trades will be routed to that firm's trading floor, and thus more commissions generated.

The typical career path for most research analysts who choose to leave that role is to go to the buy side, such as a hedge fund or other asset management firms that used to be clients that they used to call on. Some also move to venture capital firms given their expertise in a particular industry. Unlike corporate finance or M&A, research analysts are not expected to go pursue an MBA (if they don't already have one), but rather to obtain a Chartered Financial Analyst (CFA) certification.

Capital Markets

Capital Markets is essentially a hybrid between corporate finance and trading; the department connects the groups outside the wall with the groups inside the wall, hence the rationale for why straddle the Chinese wall. The division is responsible for new securities issues, whether it's an initial public offering or a follow-on offering. Capital Markets works with corporate finance when a client needs to raise money in the public markets, which could be new stocks being issued or new bonds.

Unlike analysts in corporate finance or M&A, the role for analysts in Capital Markets is less focused on corporate valuations and more on securities valuation. That sounds a bit confusing because securities valuation impacts a company's valuation, so let me clarify it this way. If you are valuing a public company the way someone in corporate finance does, you're looking at the entire company and its capital structure; you look at the equity portion and how much that's worth, and you look at how much total debt the company has outstanding to get you to the firm's value. In Capital Markets, you would be more focused on analyzing the individual series of the bonds outstanding, as well as how the stock is trading. The corporate valuation work is usually handled by the corporate finance division.

Initial public offerings (IPO) are mainly handled by Capital Markets, although usually members of the corporate finance team will also participate.   Capital Markets is much more process-oriented and less strategic focus.   Generally, analysts going into the Capital Markets division are individuals who like the markets, but don't want to do trading and do not want to put up with the extensive hours that are the epitome of corporate finance and M&A.   Hours are much more reasonable, but the career options should you decide to leave that role seem to be a bit more limited outside of the bank.   The harsh reality is that the skill sets honed in that role at the junior level are not as easily transferable, so typically analysts in that position usually try to rotate to other areas of the firm if they decide to change career paths.

Other Divisions

While it isn't necessary to explain all the other divisions that make up investment banking, a couple other areas that are worth short explanations include the following:

- **Financial Sponsors (or sometimes called Private Equity Group)** – This division is very similar to a typical corporate finance or M&A group, but the clients are private equity (PE) or leverage buyout (LBO) firms rather than traditional corporations.   Bankers pitch recapitalizations/financings, and M&A ideas to those PE and LBO firms just as bankers in other areas do to traditional corporations.   Analysts that work in these groups are natural feeders into the PE or LBO shops that are clients of the firm since they have interactions with and get to know those firms fairly well on transactions.

- **High Yield (or sometimes called Leveraged Finance)** – This division resembles the Credit division, except the clients are non-investment grade. It usually works directly with Financial Sponsors group since most PE and LBO firms issue significant amounts of debt which are non-investment grade. Similarly, analysts in this group also are natural feeder to PE and LBO firms for that reason.

- **Private Banking (Private Client Services)** – This division resembles being a broker at a typical brokerage firm where you are responsible for managing investment portfolios for clients (think Charles Schwab or AG Edwards), the main difference is that clients in these departments are much wealthier, most with minimum assets of $10 million.

- **Principal Investing or Proprietary Trading** – This division represents the internal private equity or hedge fund group for a bank. Instead of executing trades for institutional clients, this division invests the firm's own capital. The division is typically quite independent from other areas of the firm and sometimes competes with the firm's outside clients. Analysts will typically not be hired into such a group without several years of experience prior.

To conclude the explanations on the various divisions, let's walk through a simple example as a way to demonstrate the interaction of the various divisions. Let's assume that you're an analyst in the Consumers Group at J.P. Morgan. The Managing Director (MD) pitched the idea of Procter & Gamble (P&G) acquiring Kimberly Clark, both major consumer products companies, and the client P&G agrees to proceed. Since this is a major acquisition, there will be significant involvement of different groups internally. The MD will work with his counterparts in the M&A group to figure out the right strategy for executing the transaction, what regulatory issues are relevant, and valuation. As the analyst in the coverage group, you will work intimately with the analyst(s) in the other product groups, such as M&A, who has probably built the initial merger model with or without you. There will be financing topics that need to be addressed: hence, the MD will work with the counterparts in Credit and Capital Markets to determine how much debt and equity will be needed to finance the transaction. Once the optimal amount of debt or equity needed has been determined, Credit will work to syndicate (find other lenders) the bank debt amount, while Capital Markets executes the issuance of new public securities (stock and/or bonds) for the rest of the financing required. The sales team will call institutional investors to entice them to buy the newly issued public securities and traders will make a market for the new securities after it has been issued. Equity research may issue a report to opine on the strategic rationale of the transaction. While not as many departments would be involved in typical transactions that are smaller, on major ones such as in the example, it would be very typical for significant collaboration across many divisions. Clearly, the Consumer coverage group serves as the hub where the other groups are connected and handles the coordination between them, as shown in the following diagram:

Example of Interaction Between Departments

P&G to acquire Kimberly Clark

Product Groups vs. Industry Coverage Groups

Now that I've explained the key divisions within an investment banking firm, it is helpful to clarify product groups versus industry groups. The terminology is simple enough to understand the difference: industry groups are corporate finance departments that specialize on a specific sector, whereas product groups specialize on a financial product without regards to industry, generally speaking. The typical classifications for the various divisions include:

- Industry Coverage Groups – Healthcare; Financial Institutions (FIG); Consumers; Industrials; Technology; Media & Telecom

- Product Groups – M&A, Leveraged Finance, Debt Capital Markets, Equity Capital Markets

Industry coverage groups are essentially client managers and relationship owners. They have a deep understanding of the clients in their sector and bring the bankers from the product groups in when a specific client has a desire to utilize that product expertise. Good coverage bankers will have an understanding of the products as well, but typically not to the level of the product group bankers.

Depending on your preferences, there are key advantages to being in one group rather than the other. If you are very passionate about an industry, it's likely you'll be better off going into an industry group that you like since you'll get to see a variety of issues and financial products that get pitched to clients in that sector. You might as well have an interest in the sector if you're going to spend long hours working on projects related to it. You'll get to see the whole array of products and work with the product groups on those presentations and transactions. The disadvantage is that you won't be an expert on any of the products, but you'll get a good "big picture" and holistic understanding of how corporations function, as well as know the industry fairly well.

The advantage of going into product groups is that you'll develop a key expertise on the financial product, but won't know as much about a sector. If you like advisory, but have no particular industry preferences, then choosing a product group will be better, such as M&A or leveraged finance. Unfortunately, the trade-off is that if you're in a product group that you don't like, and the options available with that particular product group's skill sets are limited, switching out will be very difficult, even internally.

Timing often has an impact on the popularity of groups. Certain specialized groups such as Emerging Market Debt may be hot when those economies are doing well, but a major downturn in the market or crisis (think the Russian debt crisis, or a major governmental coup, which isn't as uncommon as one would think as one dictator replaces another in an emerging economy), the product could completely be dead as no one wants to touch it until the situation improves.   In a situation like that, you could be looking at doing a lot of thumb twiddling and pen flipping in your analyst career until the product becomes hot again.

As a general advice, if you don't have a particular preference for one sector product in particular, stick with a position that is more of a generalist role. This will allow you to get as much exposure as possible. Good bankers need to know about a variety of areas, even the specialists usually have experience in other groups prior to specializing.   That's the reason why some firms expect Associates to rotate through several groups before settling them into a particular one.   As an analyst, having a broader background will keep more options open, as well as giving you a chance to really figure out what interests you most.   Some analysts seem to think they know what they want to do when they first join, but on many an occasion, preferences change.

Bulge Bracket Firm vs. Boutique Bank

Sometimes candidates are just glad to get an investment banking offer, but for the few individuals who are lucky enough to get several offers, ranging from bulge bracket firms to boutique investment banks, the choice can be confusing. While many would argue that the decision is obvious in favor of the bulge bracket firms, I would urge you to take a step back before jumping to that conclusion.

Let's start by explaining what the differences are between the two. A bulge bracket firm is the term that refers to the large, most distinguished investment banking firms, namely Goldman Sachs, Morgan Stanley and Merrill Lynch in the original bunch, then with the addition of Citigroup (formerly Salomon Smith Barney), JP Morgan, and most recently Lehman Brothers. They have a long history and strong brand recognition. Beyond the prestige of working for a global firm, the advantages these firms have include their diverse product offerings (one-stop shop) to their clients, huge platform of resources, and typically focuses on the largest deals in the market. Most of the transactions seen in the Wall Street Journal articles or Bloomberg are essentially dominated by advisors from these firms.

Boutique investment banks (or "boutiques" for short) on the other hand are usually specialized firms. Some specialize purely in advisory (M&A), while others have sector specializations. Some boutiques offer a fairly diverse range of services to their clients that can compete with those of their bulge bracket counterparts (examples include Lazard, Jefferies and the Blackstone Group). Most boutiques tend to focus on smaller middle market transactions. While they do not have the resources and as global a platform as the bulge bracket firms, there are certain advantages that boutiques have: they are less bureaucratic, so transactions and approval processes internally tend to be much more rapid. You will get much more responsibilities working on a transaction in a boutique firm than you would at a bulge bracket firm. If you make a mistake, you can't hide, whereas in a bulge bracket firm, it's easier to do so.

Bulge Bracket vs. Boutique Firm Summary

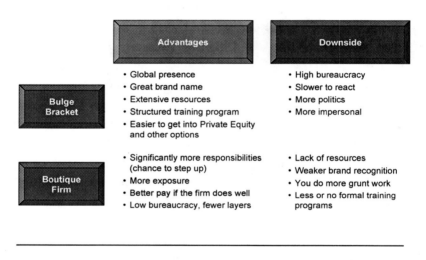

Clearly, if you have the option to choose between the two, it's helpful to understand which of the tradeoffs you are willing to make. Having had experience in both environments, my most rewarding experience as a banker had been more at the boutique firms, although having the experience at the bulge bracket firms was what helped me keep many career options open. It is much easier to switch from a bulge bracket firm into a smaller boutique firm, so that's always an option, but the other way around does not hold true. In good years, strong bankers from the boutique firms have been able to make the transition to the bulge bracket firms (assuming they want to do so), but most of the time that option proves difficult.

Ironically, most think that getting into a smaller boutique firm is easier than a bulge bracket firm, but the reality may not hold true. Boutique firms (the smaller ones in particular) don't offer training programs, so you have to be much more prepared, which means that without a finance degree or prior financial experience, your ability to add value and learn the business will be very challenging. Unless you're a very self-motivated person, it will be much harder to succeed because there are fewer people there to guide you through things and serve as a bouncing board for questions.

There are numerous firms in between the boutique banks and the bulge bracket firms, which may be a good mix of advantages between the two. The majority of people would assume the bulge bracket firm is the ideal starting ground, but if that option is not available to you, at least you can make the argument of why a boutique environment may be a good one for you during your interviews at those firms.

Ultimately, choose the firm where you feel most comfortable and where you think you'll get the most experience. If you're a very entrepreneurial person and like a smaller cozier environment, the boutique might be a better route to take. Working for the right people is much more important than working for the right firm, because they'll be the individuals who help develop and mentor you. There are people who finish up their analyst programs at the big firms with barely any good deal experience and they will likely have difficulty trying to find their next option, whereas an analyst who has had the chance to step up and execute more deals at a boutique firm can point to transaction experience that will be incomparable to his peers elsewhere.

III. Internships

Internships are truly important, no matter what others may tell you. The best way to get a full time job when you graduate is to have an internship opportunity where you have been extended an offer at the end of the summer. While I don't have any quantified research statistics, I would approximate that 75% of summer interns are extended a full time offer (in normal times) with the firms by the end of their internships and avoid the extremely competitive normal recruiting cycle. Of course, the other 25% of students who do not receive an offer face a very awkward situation when they are interviewing in the normal recruiting cycle in the fall: explaining to recruiters why they were not offered a full time position by the firms where they had interned at. Thus, it would behoove you to find an internship at a firm which may offer you a job when you graduate. And once you have the internship, you need to work smart and work hard over those 10 weeks to make sure you're one of the 75% that do get extended an offer.

How to get an Internship

Every major Wall Street investment bank has internships. Some even offer internships during the school year (Dartmouth College, for example, allows some students to take a semester off to work where they can extend their summer internship to nine months instead of the usual summer three months). That, however, is significantly rarer than conglomerate co-op positions, and tends to be unique situations that are not some formal structured internship program; this means that if you want to do this, you would need to make special arrangements and discuss it with the Human Resource (HR) person before the internship begins, and get approval from the department head of your department at the employing firm.

Internships are designed mainly for juniors entering their senior year following their summer program. However, this does not mean that you should not apply if you are a sophomore or even a freshman. In fact, some internships are designed as three-year programs which allow freshmen to be accepted and return every summer until they graduate. Unfortunately or fortunately, depending on your perspective, these programs tend to be limited to minorities and/or women.

While every recognized investment bank offers an internship, this doesn't mean that you'll be given fair chances at those internships. In an ideal world, everyone from every university will have full and fair access to those internship opportunities. The reality of the situation, however, is that if you come from a top school and have the right connections, you may be able to leverage that relationship into a summer internship opportunity much more easily than someone from an average school. Ironically, if you call up the Human Resource department of some of the investment banks, they may even tell you that they don't offer formal summer internships. Firms like J.P. Morgan, Goldman Sachs, Credit Suisse First Boston (CSFB), Morgan Stanley, and Citigroup all have fairly large (relatively speaking) summer internship programs. Get in touch with the HR department of those firms to make sure you submit your resume on time. The Career Services Center at your university should have that information; if not, you should not be hesitant to contact the companies directly about their recruiting schedule and deadlines. Absolutely do not miss the deadlines.

All the major Wall Street firms will have recruiting presentations on campus of the top 20 universities, which are excellent opportunities to get to know people at the firm and start the networking process. To kick off the normal recruiting cycle for fulltime hires, the presentations are usually done at the beginning of fall; summer internship recruiting presentations are usually done in the spring, if at all. Use that opportunity to also learn about the companies, write down notes specific about each company that you are interested in so that you can customize it in your cover letter when you submit your resume. Each individual that you meet who you had a good conversation with, send them a thank you email or letter to get your name in front of them; then follow up with a call if you were able to get their number. There are thousands and thousands of resumes submitted to these limited internship opportunities, so you need to find a way to get your name to stand out. If there's an alumni you know at the company, don't hesitate to call them to get the inside scoop; the worse case scenario is that they don't return your call and may be a little irritated. However, the upside is so worth it; they may even offer to pass your resume on to the appropriate person and put in a good word for you for taking the initiative.

Do not be shy about asking for internships when you are talking to a representative or alumni from the various firms that are presenting at your school during the normal fulltime recruiting presentations. They have been in your position before, so they can empathize and will at least let you know what the process is for internship recruiting. I remember feeling awkward bringing it up myself when I was looking for internships; it seemed like all the representatives at the presentations were only interested in prospects for hiring fulltime, so you get the run-around; back then, most firms did not host internship recruiting presentations so it was even tougher to get their attention. You should target the HR people first; they usually make themselves known at the presentations early on and will let you know what the process is and the schedules are for internship recruiting. Don't take it personally or get frustrated if people seem disinterested, they just have a different schedule for internship recruiting and rightly or wrongly, they know they will have another chance to talk to you next year as a full time candidate so they want to limit their attention to the best candidates that they want to hire fulltime in the coming recruiting cycle.

Check the companies' websites. With the Internet becoming so commonly used as a medium of information distribution, much of the recruiting information can be found on each company's website. You can even submit your resume online now; when I was an undergraduate, even though email was starting to be more prominent, HR people still expected resumes and cover letters to be on hard copies on nice bond paper. Now, it's probably more efficient and there's much less lead time required to have the resume and cover letter ready and sent out by email instead.

Other Networking Opportunities

If you were not lucky enough to land a summer internship, you can get a head start on the networking process by attending some of the summer networking events, most are based in New York City. Even if you do end up getting a summer internship, it would be useful to take advantage of the summer networking opportunities since it will also allow you to share insights and experiences about the firm you work at with others who are working at other firms. Most events are free or relatively cheap if there is cost; just make sure there are no RSVP requirements where you have to get yourself onto a guest list in advance.

Women on Wall Street (WOWS) is a networking organization started by a former senior female investment banker with the intent of fostering networking opportunities and support for women of Wall Street…and potential future women looking to enter Wall Street.   The organization hosts summer events and annual conferences that provide ample opportunities to get connected if you fit the membership criteria.   Since I am a guy and didn't fit the criteria, I can't speak much about that organization without personal experience, but I do have some friends that are in the network and they speak highly of the events.

Some investment banks will also host school-specific events during the summer.   This is their way of trying to have their summer interns entice interns at other banks or non-banking firms to explore opportunities with them.   Ask HR or people you know that are currently working at the firms you're interested in to see if there are summer recruiting events geared towards your school and get on their mailing lists so that you are notified of when and where they are hosted.

A well-kept secret that some interns and recent graduates try not to publicize (or are simply not aware of) is that the Yale Club of New York City also hosts its "Young Alumni and Friends" cocktail events over the summer to allow young alumni and their friends to network over the summer.   Although the Yale Club's intent was to foster networking opportunities for its younger alumni network in New York City, the reality is that you do not have to be a member to attend the summer events.   The events are on Thursday evenings from 6:00 pm – 8:30 pm beginning near the end of June through the first week of August; you can check the schedule on the website (http://www.yaleclubnyc.com) just to make sure when they are.   Other university-affiliated clubs may have networking events over the summer as well, but this one is the most well-attended and open to non-members. Just make sure not to wear jeans and t-shirts, they will and do enforce dress codes!

Minority Internships

If you are a minority, you already know the countless obstacles you have to overcome to get an internship, let alone an internship on Wall Street.   Fortunately, there are two minority internships that make being a minority truly a significant advantage.   I briefly describe them both but more information can be obtained from the specific organizations themselves through their website or contacting them directly.

Sponsors for Educational Opportunity (SEO)

If you are a minority, there is clearly no better summer internship program to participate in than the Sponsors for Educational Opportunity (SEO) Career Program for getting into Wall Street. This is absolutely the best Wall Street internship program out there, bar none.   The reason is simple: no other Wall Street internship will give you as much exposure and access to all the major firms than this program does simply because of the way the Career Program is structured and the relationship history that SEO has with every major Wall Street firm.   The founder of the program, Michael Osheowitz, was a former investment banker himself, who established the organization in 1962 as a mentorship program to give students of color exposure and access that had been unprecedented prior to its establishment.

SEO's Career Program has grown significantly since its inception in the early 1980s. Even though the program started with approximately ten people in its initial program in Investment Banking, today, the class size has grown to over four hundred across all of the areas that SEO offers internships in. In addition to investment banking, the organization also offers career internships in corporate law, asset management, accounting, and most recently added philanthropy; management consulting used to be a program that was offered, but was discontinued over the past couple years along with the media program that was unsuccessfully launched. While most of the internships are based in New York City, SEO's Career Program has expanded domestically as well as internationally with its alumni base of approximately 3,500. It is arguably the most powerful minority network on Wall Street where alumni continue to serve and help the organization grow and evolve.

SEO's Career Program recruits, interviews, and accepts exceptional minority students into the program and then places those students in various firms on Wall Street, depending on which Career Program the student was accepted into. You do not get a choice of which firm you will be placed at. However, due to the way the Career Program is structured, each of the major firms that take SEO interns will host a reception over the summer with representatives from various departments and recruiters; thus, regardless of which firm you work at, you will be given an opportunity to network at those receptions with other firms. SEO will also provide a week-long training, more appropriately and endearingly termed "boot camp," to prepare its interns for their internships, and each intern will also be provided an alumni mentor as well as a mentor at their firm. Furthermore, at the end of the summer, SEO interns are offered interviews before they return to their school. Lastly, but perhaps just as importantly, the program pays interns quite well.

Not surprisingly, the Career Program is highly competitive and having the highest GPA or SAT/LSAT scores are not enough. Each year, thousands apply for very limited positions available. When I was in the Asset Management Program, there were only ten spots available. Investment Banking is by far the largest program with over 200 people when I was a participant. The number of slots available varies by year depending on economic conditions and participating firms' willingness to take interns.

The Career Program accepts qualified individuals who are well-rounded both academically and socially (for example, volunteering and providing community services) that have faced and overcome significant challenges in their background. Stereotypically, an SEO Career Program intern will have good academic credentials, volunteering and social services background, leadership experience, and a strong desire to succeed and give back. The best way to get into the program is to talk to alumni of the Career Program at your school and learn as much as you can about the program. The application should be taken almost as seriously, if not more so, than a college application; reviewers are anally brutal with mistakes that they find on the application. The most important part is getting offered an interview and surviving that 45-minute interview. In the past, the interviews were only 15 minutes long and intended to be a pressure cooker experience, but in recent years, they have become more humane and resemble traditional interviews on Wall Street.

If you qualify as a minority and you are interested in a Wall Street internship, you would be doing yourself a huge disservice by not applying to the SEO Career Program. Even if you are not a junior, you should apply and if you don't get in the first time, you can still reapply the year after. If you were offered an SEO internship versus another internship, you would be much better off accepting the SEO internship.

More information about the SEO program can be found on the organization's website (http://www.seo-usa.org).

INROADS, Inc.

This minority internship organization resembles the SEO Career Program. Although it lacks the prestige that SEO's Career Program has with the major Wall Street firms, one of the advantages of the INROADS program is that it is longer term. Freshmen are offered the opportunity to return each summer to the internship program, so you get to build a very strong network with the company that you are interning at over the various summers that you spend there. In contrast, SEO is mainly a one-shot deal and it is unusual to get a second SEO internship after having gone through the program once unless you applied to a different sub-program (for example, you did Accounting one year and then applied to Investment Banking the next). Another advantage of the INROADS program is that there are more options to consider; while SEO if focused mainly on finance and law careers at the major firms, INROADS also offers programs in general corporations as well, such as Coca Cola.

There are some INROADS interns who apply and switch into the SEO Career Program after they reach their junior year, mainly due to the networking opportunities offered by SEO's events.

Richard B. Fisher Scholar Program

This is an internship program specifically at Morgan Stanley also designed to improve diversity. Even though Morgan Stanley is a major sponsor of the SEO Career Program, they continue to have Fisher Scholars. Over the summer, Fisher Scholars will also participate in the special events at Morgan Stanley that are intended for SEO interns. However, like the INROADS program, it does not provide the other key benefits offered by SEO's Career Program of attending receptions hosted by other firms, the boot camp training, and the early interviews at the end of the summer. Nevertheless, it is a good internship to consider.

In addition to Morgan Stanley, other firms are also offering summer diversity internships outside the usual SEO and INROADS internship opportunities with an emphasis on minorities and women. Citigroup and UBS are two of those firms. To find out for sure which firms do, you should check the companies' websites to start with, and then call up HR to make sure you know what the requirements are as well as the application process. Some are just geared towards sophomores without specific demographic criteria such as the CSFB Sophomore Rotational Program where you spend 2-3 weeks in various departments to get a sense of what they do; those programs usually lead to an offer to return as a junior intern the following summer.

IV. Interviews

Your resume will get you into the door, but it's the interviews that will get you through it. In this section, I hope to help explain some of the key things that interviewers look for, and what are the things that you should be prepared for.

Getting the Interviews

Before we get to how to prepare for an interview, let's start by trying to get an interview in the first place. Getting a job on Wall Street is extremely tough, although relatively easier during economic boom periods. But even during good economic cycles, the jobs are still fairly limited. While I don't have the hard statistics to confirm this, my past involvement with recruiting and working with HR on their recruitment efforts, I would estimate with reasonable certainty that approximately 50% of the jobs have already been filled after the summer internships by those interns given offers to return. A typical investment banking class at one of the larger firms, say Citigroup, will have approximately 100-150 analysts who will get placed into the various global offices of the firm's corporate finance groups (doesn't include Sales & Trading). This means that only 50-75 slots are still available to be filled. As for those graduating from an MBA program, the number of Associate slots are even fewer, by approximately a third. If you think about how many schools there are, multiplied by the number of students that are applying versus how many slots there are across Wall Street, the odds are fairly intimidating.

Getting an interview is probably one of the hardest parts of landing an investment banking job, and the sad part is that it's not always fair. You can be the most qualified person and still not get an interview, and yet someone who doesn't meet the typical credentials may get an interview that you feel you deserve, maybe because they know someone on the inside, or their parent happens to be the CEO of a client that the investment bank does business with. Life isn't fair, and the odds are stacked pretty much against you. However, there are some basic things that will help you improve your odds. Hopefully reading this guide will level the playing field a bit.

Major investment banking firms have become more systematic in the way they recruit and you need to make sure you are fully aware of the process. For example, Citigroup's recruiting for investment banking is like a machine in absolute efficiency on the process; the organization and structure of the process makes it even more fundamentally crucial that you don't miss certain steps. There are essentially no second chances when you've missed the process, no matter what sob story you come up with. Attention to detail is one of the key skill sets that are sought by hiring managers for new analysts, so missing the recruiting process is not something they would consider a good start.

Here are some key things to do:

1. Know the dates and deadlines – Know the recruiting schedule for the firms you want to interview with; this will help you prioritize and prepare. It's absolutely crucial that you don't miss deadlines. You can try calling HR, but most likely you're not going to get a hold of them, so your best bet is to check in with your Career Services department at your school. They will usually have a schedule of all the firms visiting to give a recruiting presentation with the respective dates,

locations, etc. Some firms will have separate departments give separate presentations on your campus (Sales & Trading typically run recruiting separate from Corporate Finance), so if there are particular areas that you're interested in, make sure you go to the right presentation.

2. Know what you need to submit. Some firms will expect a cover letter, resume, and transcript at the same time; while others expect only a resume and cover letter initially. Some will only accept resume books from your career services office, but some expect you to submit the resumes directly through the firm's website. A few firms such as Barclays Capital actually do recruiting slightly differently: they require a test (similar to the SAT) to be taken as a preliminary screen, so you have to make sure you know the specific date of the exam and where it's hosted; while this is rather tedious, the consolation is that the top scorer gets a $10K prize.

3. Attend the recruiting presentations of the visiting firms – This is a great way to get your name out there so they can put a face to your resume when they see it; furthermore, it's a great networking opportunity, not to mention free food. Collect business cards and try to follow up with a thank-you email or phone call; you may not get a response, but it'll keep your name on their radar screen. Doesn't take more than a few minutes but it can have a big impact on your future, so those few minutes are well worth investing in.

4. Check and recheck your resume and cover letters– Every year, in every resume books that I've reviewed there is inevitably several resumes with typos on them. Only in rare occasions do people overlook that, and it makes a bad first impression. The same applies to cover letters. When you're writing a cover letter to the Recruiter for Goldman Sachs, don't address it to the Recruiter for Citigroup on the header…yes, I have seen that happen! Interestingly, the recruiters at the various firms seem to know who each other are, and they recognize those names. Another funny anecdote is when I saw one candidate's cover letter addressed to Citigroup, but in the body, the text read "CSFB is the premier investment bank that I want to work for." Needless to say, he wasn't offered an interview at Citigroup. It's very easy to miss basic typos especially after long nights of partying or schoolwork, so make sure you let a friend or someone else check it before submitting your information.

5. Leverage your former classmates – If there are people who are just a year or two ahead of you working at those firms, don't be shy and call them up. Ask the Career Services department if they can refer you to an alumni working at any of the firms you're interested in. Those are your best contacts, and most likely to want to help you out. Guess who are the main people reviewing the resume books that are submitted to the firms, other than HR? That's right, the analysts who were a year or two ahead of you. Sure there are associates and others that may review the resume books as well, but the brunt of it comes down to the analysts, especially the ones that are

from your school. Because they are familiar with the school and the courses, they are in the best position to know an easy course versus a real tough course, so they can best evaluate the candidates in the resume books from their respective schools. Graduates from schools like NYU and Georgetown have phenomenal loyalty and do a great job of preparing potential candidates from those schools. I remember during a discussion when we had been discussing candidates from Yale, one of the individual's credentials were slightly below average for the standards we expected and would have been omitted for an interview, but an analyst who knew the individual well was able to convince the rest of the group to bring that candidate in for an interview nevertheless.

6. Do your research – Try to know a little about the firms that are visiting campus. That way, you won't be like every other student trying to get an interview and can ask intelligent questions when you are chatting up some of the representatives from the firms.

Some Pointers on Resumes

The resume should be one-page, clearly laying out your academic as well as professional achievements. If you don't have much work experience (it's ok, most people don't coming out of an undergraduate program), you will likely have to find ways to highlight achievements and skills that imply you are an overachiever, smart, hardworking and have good leadership potential. Some basic things to remember:

•   Fonts – Don't use more than three different font sizes and stick with normal business fonts (Times, Arial, Courier, etc…no funky calligraphy styles), keep the font big enough so the reader isn't straining to read your accomplishments (11 point Times Roman font would be pushing it).

- Be concise and use action verbs when describing your points (bullet points work well); stick with 2-3 bullet points per section of the resume.

- Prioritize your points by putting the most important items first.

- Check and recheck your documents before sending them out; you may have different drafts and versions of your resume for different types of jobs, just make sure you're sending out the right ones to the right people

- Convert to Acrobat PDF format – While not crucial, this is useful because how you see the document on the screen will be exactly how it will come out when printed by the reader; sometimes when you leave a document in MS Word or other word processing program format, the pagination and formatting changes based on the reader's printer settings.

- Headers – This is the top part of most resumes where you have your contact information.   Make sure to include your phone number (ideally use your cell phone number if you have one) and your email address. Something that is important to note is that the email address should be something that sounds normal and professional (johndoe@)yahoo.com). If you don't have one, just create one on Yahoo, Gmail, or Hotmail for free. As obvious as that may sound, I have seen resumes with "hotlips69" or "tulips82" as the candidate's email identity; not only will you likely not get considered seriously, but your emails will likely be blocked by the spam filtering system at most of the investment banking firms and the anticipated recipient would not even get it.

- Format – Keep it simple and professional. You want to stand out for your achievements, not for how creative your resume looks. Some people get suspicious when they see an overly ornate format because they think the candidate has something to hide. The candidate may simply be very artistic and creative, but that's not what the interviewer is particularly looking for in a candidate. An investment banking resume is very different from a resume for a marketing job.

Many books exist on how to write a good resume and provide sample templates. If you have never created a resume, it's best to start one as soon as possible since they tend to go through numerous iterations. Some career service offices offer free consultation services and feedback on resumes, so you should use them but don't wait until the last minute if you need a quick turnaround.

A Few Comments on Cover Letters

Some people find cover letters useful, but if interviewers are anything like me when I evaluate a candidate, I very rarely read them and just jump right to the resume. What's the point of cover letters? It's sole purpose is to get people to read your resume, not more, nothing less. With that in mind, there are a few things to keep in mind when writing cover letters.

- Keep it short and sweet – One page is the limit, never write a two-page cover letter that will most likely not be read.

- Limit it to about 3-4 paragraphs at most – As a recruiter, I'd expect you to:

    1) Tell me who you are (name drop if you know someone at the firm that can recommend you or remind me of how/when we met) (the introduction);

    2) Tell me what makes you special and a fit for the position you are applying for compared to everybody else (the body of the letter); and

    3) Thank me for reviewing/considering you (the closing).

- Highlight the most important points on the resume that you'd want someone to notice.

- Always check for grammatical and spelling errors, not to mention to make sure you are addressing it to the right person.

- Have someone else read it before you send it out.

When recruiters review a cover letter, they spend less than 5 minutes usually, so if you don't get them excited, chances are you will be passed over to the next candidate unless your resume is strong. Most of the time, people just go right to the resume anyways and skip the cover letter.

Preparing for Interviews

There are numerous books out there on how to prepare for interviews, so I won't rewrite much of the advice that's already out there. Ultimately, preparation is key to making you stand out in a positive way. If the career service center at your school offers it, you should take advantage of the practice interviews. For example, the Yale Career Services Center offers videotaping of mock interviews for free so you can watch yourself and be critiqued. Very few students take advantage of such a valuable resource (myself included when I was a student). Another very useful resource is asking anyone you know who are currently investment bankers to help you go through practice interviews. And if neither of those resources are available to you, the very least you should do is ask a friend to go through practice interview questions. While it may not be as ideal, at the very least it will help you get used to answering interview questions.

What Do Interviewers Look For?

While each specific division will have differences in their prototypes of what their ideal candidate is, there are certain consistencies that make a candidate worth considering.

- **Intellect** – In the advisory business, people will only consider your advice if they think you're smart, so it's not surprising that this is a key component that interviewers look for. Generally speaking, there are minimum GPA levels that are considered cut-off levels when filtering out resumes. Barring unique circumstances (such as special connections), most major Wall Street firms will have a minimum GPA cut-off at 3.0, although the majority of candidates typically have average GPAs of 3.5+ from good schools. High SAT and GMAT scores are also typically included as consideration. Quantitative skills are particularly important, so make sure to highlight any particular examples where you demonstrate proficiency in this area.

- **Leadership Potential** – Not surprisingly, leadership involvement in extra-curricular activities helps. Overachievers are typically in those roles. Investment banking is a high strung business dominated by Type A personalities.

- **Teamwork** – While leadership quality is important, so is teamwork effectiveness. Interviewers will probe for this by looking at the types of extra-curricular activities you are involved with. If all your time is spent reading, perhaps that may imply you're smart but it also says you're a loner. This isn't going to fly because being antisocial is not going to get you very far in business, and certainly less so on Wall Street. An interview may also probe for teamwork (and leadership) by asking you to give an example of a group project you did and your role on that project, sort of a psychological profile.

- **Work Experience** – This is something that's harder for someone coming out of an undergraduate program who typically only has a couple internships rather than real work experience, which is why the internships are so important junior year. If you had worked at an investment bank, this will significantly improve your odds, assuming you had good reviews. The reason is simple: investment banking is a tough job, so until you've done it, they don't know if you can really handle it. Thus, the odds improve dramatically if someone's already done it before. It sounds unfair for someone just trying to get in, sort of a chicken and the egg situation…you can't get in because you don't have the experience, but you don't have the experience because you can't get in. Unfortunately, that's how the business world works, and while there are things beyond your control, you can at least try to improve the odds on factors that are within your control (i.e., trying to develop relationships and connections).

- **Business Sense** – Similar to the psychological profiling for teamwork and leadership capacity, interviewers will look for people with a good business sense. This is often tested with questions about a business case study: for example, they may ask you to walk you through the key factors you would think about when starting up a pet store (or whatever store). While there isn't a set correct answer, the interviewer is probing to understand your thought process, much like the case interviews done by consulting companies. I would recommend checking out the websites for some of the strategy consulting firms (bcg.com, mckinsey.com, monitor.com and mercer.com) that have posted sample case studies on their website.

- **Cultural Fit** – Birds of a feather flock together, as the saying goes. People like working with people who are similar to them. This is has been statistically tested and proven to hold true in many studies. Thus, the interviewer has to "like" you and think you fit into the culture of the firm and/or department. Unfortunately, it's hard to understand how this is measured or fits in until you've worked at the various firms. Not all investment banking firms are the same, some have more distinct cultures than others. For example, Goldman Sachs has generally been known as a more team-oriented environment where you put the team first above all else (including your personal life) rather than valuing superstars, balanced with bigger egos. In contrast, Bear Stearns has a reputation for a tougher environment with more cut-throat self-preservation mentality that values superstars. Unfortunately despite these generalizations, each department will also vary with its own cultures, and chances are, you won't know until you're working with them. The best and only way to know is to ask people who are working there to get their impressions. Then you can try and tailor your responses to match the culture of the group or firm: don't go into a Goldman Sachs interview and claim you'll be the superstar!

- **Ability to Multitask and Handle Stress** – Lastly, but certainly just as importantly, the ability to multitask and handle stress is a key trait of successful bankers. If you can't handle stress, chances are, this is a job that you won't last very long in. I remember having a coworker named Sergio from Stanford that was in my Analyst Program at JP Morgan; after less than six months into the job, he resigned and moved back to California because he was rapidly balding and couldn't handle the stress. Whether it's a physical or mental thing, you need to be able to demonstrate that you have successfully handled multiple projects simultaneously (again, it goes back to having a good academic record combined with significant involvement in extra-curricular activities).

While I've listed key traits that are sought by interviewers, only a few will have all the traits and fit the mold perfectly. If you're not one of those individuals, your objective should be to highlight the strongest areas where you shine, and minimize the areas where you're weak during the interviews. This comes with good interviewing skills, which is a function of practice and experience. Some useful things to keep in mind:

- **Strong, firm handshake** – This takes two seconds at most, and yet is usually the first factor of an initial impression. You're not trying to break the bones in the interviewers fingers, but don't let your hands limp into theirs waiting for them to keep it up for you.

- **Show confidence, not arrogance** – You should be confident of your abilities and should speak with confidence when you respond to an interviewer, with that said, you don't want to sound pretentious either. Most people have met and work with some incredibly bright people, so it's not very likely you will impress them that much.

- **Look straight into the interviewers' eyes** – For most people this is certainly not the easiest thing to do. In Asian cultures, it's a sign of disrespect, but in banking and most other job interviews, it's a show of confidence.

Practice staring at yourself in the mirror or even your friends. If you still have a hard time with that, the thing that seems to work for some people is to stare at the bridge of nose...it's hard to differentiate when someone is looking at your eyes or your nose, so that's close enough and they won't know.

- **Smell good** – Sounds like dating, right? The last thing you want to do is turn someone off by having bad body odor. Invariably, most people will sweat when they're nervous, which augments the body odor; so wear deodorant, cologne or perfume (in moderation, don't bathe in it). Body odor also includes your breath, so bring breath mints! Some people prefer gum, but the problem with gum is that you have to dispose of it and may not get the opportunity to do so right before an interview. Just like dating, bad breath could kill the first impression.

I'll tell you a funny situation a couple years ago when I was volunteering to interview a candidate for the SEO Investment Banking Program (see description in the Internships chapter about the program). The candidate was a minority woman from a very good school, a junior looking for a summer internship. The interview was conducted in one of the cluttered SEO managers' offices, which was literally about the size of a tiny cubicle 4 feet by 6 feet in dimension so we were pretty scrunched together. I was partnered with one of the SEO career staff members in interviewing her simultaneously. Since it was still very early spring, the window was closed and the heater was on full blast.

Immediately when the candidate sat down and closed the office door, there was a very pungent odor that permeated the office within the first minute. Unfortunately the ventilation system was horrible, but to maintain privacy when we interviewed her (other interviewees were waiting outside), we had to keep the door closed. Without being too graphic, imagine a smell that combined a very strong curry-like scent with dirty laundry (or the smell of clothes left in the washing machine for more than a day and forgotten to be put into the dryer after it's been washed) that was exacerbated by the sweat because she was nervous and sweating profusely! I literally pretended to scratch my nose throughout the interview because I was trying to cover my nose when I breathed in. Although the interview was supposed to last 45 minutes, we were done within 25 minutes...gasping for the air outside the office after she left. My co-interviewer and I didn't even have to discuss it, we looked at each other and said immediately "No!" because the candidate literally stunk! Fortunately it was not merely the odor, but her qualifications were at best average relative to other candidates, so the decision was easy to make.

- **Write thank-you emails** – Always write an email to thank the interviewer for his or her time. It doesn't have to be anything lengthy, but it's the thought that counts.

What is the Typical Recruiting Process Like?

The recruiting process for the major investment banks is fairly similar across the board. Most have given offers to interns that were working for them over the summer, and those offers have an early acceptance date, probably in October or November at the latest. As a way to entice the early acceptance, the intern will receive a signing bonus if the offer is accepted by that date; otherwise there is a drop dead (January or February) date when the offer will expire. If you are an intern that has received an offer, and you know that you will likely accept the offer, then the signing bonus ($5-$10K) is a nice benefit to just sign by the earlier date. If you are hesitant to accept the offer and prefer to interview with other firms as well, then it may well be worth forgoing the early signing bonus. Having an existing offer dramatically increases your chances of getting an offer with another firm. The simple explanation for this is that if another firm thinks you're good enough for them (say Morgan Stanley offers you a job after the summer internship), chances are, you're just as qualified to work for the firm you're interviewing at.

When you drop your resume off with the Career Services Office at your school, that resume book is sent to the HR folks at the respective firms. Those recruiters then distribute it to the team of bankers that lead the effort for your school ("school team"). Most of the team members will likely be alumni of your school if you're from a school that is well-represented. If your school is not one where the firm typically recruits from, you'll likely have to be much more proactive because the resume drop process may not exist; this means contacting HR directly or finding an alumna who currently works at the firm to push your cause forward.

The school team then reviews the book to select the initial group of candidates that they want to interview. One of the firms I had worked at, the Yale resume book had approximately 150 candidates for corporate finance; the total number selected to be interviewed was 15 candidates, with 5 as backups should any of the 15 decide to cancel, so approximately 10%. The first rounds of interviews are usually held on campus, and the candidates are then narrowed down to about a third, depending on how strong the candidates are. Those final third will then be invited to interview at the firm's office for a full-day of interviews, what is called Super Saturdays (or Super Fridays if it's held on a Friday...they used to be held only on Saturdays but since getting volunteers to commit to coming in on a weekend to do interviews became more difficult, they introduced Super Fridays to give bankers some flexibility).

When you're invited in for a Super Saturday, the firm will usually pay for your trip and make arrangements for your housing. Typically you would arrive on a Friday, have dinner with some of the analysts that wine and dine you along with other candidates, and then you'd have the interviews the following day. This is an opportunity to get a sense of the firm's culture because you can ask the analysts the questions outside of a normal interview context. It's also a chance for you to make a good impression; the individuals at the dinner may like you so much that they make a comment to the recruiter which may have positive impact; of course, if you're a total buffoon, the opposite effect can also happen.

The Super Saturdays usually consists of four to six interviews, each 30-45 minutes long. The "pod" of interviews will consist of interviewers ranging from third year analysts to managing directors, each interviewing 4-6 candidates. The way the interviews are structured may be a bit different across firms. Some firms will have a very targeted and structured approach to interviews; for example, Citigroup's interviews have very specific areas of focus that each interviewer is supposed to try to extract from the candidate, which may or may not be obvious during the interviews. In other words, one interviewer might try to focus on your quantitative and analytical skills while another interviewer is responsible for evaluating your leadership potential, teamwork, among other categories. They will award points for each category, and those with the highest points at the end of the interview rounds in each pod will usually get an offer; the second or third highest candidates from each pod will then have to be discussed in a room full of other interviewers including those from other pods. The votes are tallied and at the end of the day, and final decisions made. Sometimes the discussions can get fairly vocal as alumni from certain schools try to get their candidates in.

Candidates will likely hear back fairly quickly after the Super Saturday, within a week at the latest. Most likely, you will get a phone call from an alumna, if not from HR, to inform you of the decision. If you have been offered a position, most likely there will be a timeframe that you need to respond to the offer by, often referred to as an "exploding offer" because they want to lock you in and prevent you from interviewing with other firms.

Once you have the written offer, the ball is in your court and the firm will put out the red carpet to woo you to sign the offer letter. They will have alumni at the firm call you to offer advice, and arrange "sell day" events in which you will be offered the opportunity to meet with other people who will try to "sell you" into believing why you should accept their offer. If you are considering other firms, you can expedite the interview process by informing them of your exploding offer situation; when the offer is from a reputable firm, they will most likely accommodate your timeframe and try to arrange interviews for you outside the normal timeframe.

What are Some Typical Interview Questions?

This is not a comprehensive list of questions, but you should be prepared to answer these questions as they tend to be fairly generic and often pop up. Despite all my harping on being prepared, I should clarify that the answers should not be memorized. Nothing sounds more irritating than hearing a candidate regurgitate canned responses that they had memorized. A good interview is one where you feel like you're enjoying a conversation rather than robotic responsiveness like a Jeopardy game.

Here is a list of some questions that you may be asked at interviews:

- Why do you want to do investment banking? (Don't say it's because of the money, that's an absolute no no! This is merely a question to test if you know what investment banking is.)

- What department would you like to be in? Do you have a preference? (This is sometimes a factor for recruiting because certain years, there are too many candidates only interested in a specific sector, so if you say you have experience in a particular group that is more esoteric and have an interest in focusing on that, it could be to your advantage. The objective is to let them know you're open to various options, rather than saying you're only willing to accept a certain department (unless of course you really are that adamant about it and you have already received another offer that essential guarantees you into a specific group.)

- What are some quantitative courses you've taken and how did you do in them?

- Describe a situation where you worked on a group project and your role.

- Tell me what you think your greatest weakness is. (It's a trick question, you're supposed to say something like "I am a hard worker and sometimes forget to take time to rest." Always try to turn a negative trait into something positive, whatever you consider your weakness to be.)

- In your last job (internship), what would your manager say about you? (This is an opportunity to highlight your strengths.)

- Describe a challenge/difficulty you faced in the past and how had you overcome it?

- Describe a situation where you've disagreed with someone about something and how did you change their minds?

- Think about a business that you would like to start and tell me the things you would think about when deciding how to get it started. (This is usually a case study type of question, so brushing up on how to answer those types of questions will help you structure your response. In questions like these, there are no "right" answers, the interviewer just wants to know how you think. Always take a few minutes to think, write down the main areas you want to focus on, and be structured/organized when you respond.)

- Where did the Dow/Nasdaq Indices closed yesterday? (If you tell them you are passionate about the stock market, you should know!)

- Explain the three financial statements and how they are interrelated.

- Why do you want to work here? Why here as opposed to another firm? (Test to see if you've done your research about the firm.)

- Why would you choose our firm over the other offer you have received?

- What makes a stock a good investment?

- What do you do for fun?

- What other jobs are you considering?

- Why did you choose to attend your university?

- What's the decimal value of 1/8?

- Why should you be selected over another candidate?

In addition to these generic questions, some interviewers (particularly in trading), may give you a brain teaser. There are guides out there now that provide sample brain teasers. The purpose of the brain teasers is to test how well you react to situations under stress and whether you can think on your feet.

Path to Wall Street

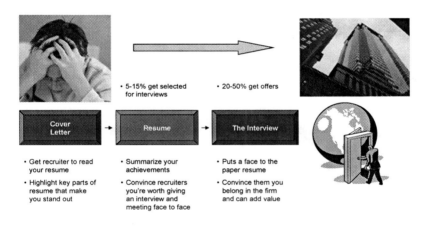

Cover Letter	Resume	The Interview
• 5-15% get selected for interviews		• 20-50% get offers

• Get recruiter to read your resume

• Highlight key parts of resume that make you stand out

• Summarize your achievements

• Convince recruiters you're worth giving an interview and meeting face to face

• Puts a face to the paper resume

• Convince them you belong in the firm and can add value

V. The Analyst Program

Now that you're in, there are some important things to keep in mind to make your experience a good one. This section focuses on the corporate finance divisions, since most of my experience has been in this area.   The analyst program is traditionally a two-year program. Most analysts are expected to stay for that period, although there are always exceptions. These days, with so many options out there, more and more analysts are leaving before their two year programs are up.

The Summer Training

After you've accepted an offer, some firms will send you "homework" in the spring as you prepare to start your Analyst program. Most of the pre-work will prove useful for those who are not finance majors as it will provide an introduction that you can do at your own pace. You will be liable to completing the assignments before you start the actual training program in the summer.

Most firms will start their training program in July that lasts for approximately ten weeks. During those ten weeks, you will be exposed to all facets of investment banking.   There will be homework that you will have to do, and exams to make sure you've learned the topics covered. These training sessions are usually taught by the firm's bankers or outside consultants, including some MBA professors. If you have no exposure to finance before, this will be a fast-paced boot camp that can prove stressful and overwhelming. You should try to review the pre-work in advance.

Topics covered in the summer training include:

- Financial modeling and how to become an Excel guru

- Accounting

- The firm's organizational structure, culture, and general propaganda of what makes the firm great so you can feel proud to be a part of it

- Overview of the company's various divisions, their roles and products

- Contacts and resources (who to call and where to find things)

- Tricks of the trade and best practices (usually taught by third year analysts)

In addition to being exposed to the various financial topics and learning about the firm and its products, the training program also serves another very important purpose: networking. This is the chance for you to get to know your classmates, they will be the ones you will be contacting for information or help during the late nights. Throughout the summer training program, HR will arrange nightly events, dinners, parties, boat cruises, etc. These events are meant to allow you to bond with your fellow classmates. As most analysts will confirm, the summer training period is probably the best period of an analyst's career since no time in the rest of your banking career will you be as pampered over such a long period.

Unless the firm you've accepted an offer from hires directly into a particular department, the training program over the summer also serves another purpose for most firms: placement. Each department will get to make a pitch during the summer to attract analysts to join their group; some departments will host cocktails or dinners as well to woo analysts. By the end of the training program, analysts are asked to rank the departments that they want to join, picking their top five choices. Each department will have an allocation of analysts, and they will tell the HR department their list of top picks in the analyst pool, ranked in order. How you perform on the exams will have a big impact on how you get placed. If you did well on an exam, and the group you ranked as #1 on your preference also ranks you as one of their tops picks, you will most likely get into that group. There is significant politics involved when negotiating which analysts get into which groups behind the scenes; the staffers will likely negotiate between themselves and HR to get certain analysts in exchange for giving up others on their preference list. The amount of behind the scene negotiations significantly resembles the NBA/NFL draft!

If you are very focused on getting into certain departments, make sure you include them in the top three. There is a danger that analysts don't realize. Certain departments that are typically harder to get into (such as M&A), if you rank them lower than #2 on your preferences will automatically drop you from their consideration. If you had interned in the department, your chances of getting into the group again after the training program should improve, if you specifically mention that you intend to return. Analysts who are already working in the departments that you want to get into often sniff out the trainees to make sure they know who are genuinely interested in their groups versus the ones who are just positioning themselves...they will be the ones at the cocktail events or taking the trainees to lunch. One way to position yourself with a department you really want to get into is to contact people there, tour the floor and talk to the staffer to express your strong interest.

What Should I Focus on When Picking a Department?

This will differ depending on the individual. My advice to most analysts that have come to me with that question is figure out what you're trying to get out of your analyst program. Are you looking to go to business school? Planning to go to private equity? Planning to go to business development? If you don't know what you want to do, then you should pick the option that keeps more doors open. As I mentioned earlier, certain groups such as capital markets will limit your options more than others. There are always trade-offs to consider. Some factors to focus on:

- Do you like the people, in particular the analysts and associates since those are the ones you'll be interacting with most? Meet as many people as you can, make sure you feel comfortable with them. Are they the type who will mentor you? Or is there a high asshole factor?

- Is there deal flow? The best experience as an analyst is being on live deals. If the department gets a few live deals and mostly does pitches, your experience will not likely be very exciting and the learning curve won't be as steep. Not having live deal will also seriously limit your future options.

- How important is quality of life to you? While in general, banking is a business of long hours, working a

12-hour day is not so bad when compared to a 16-hour day…consistently.

- Where do most analysts in the department go after they complete their two years? This is a good indicator of the caliber and prestige of the department, both internally and externally.

- How many analysts stay for the full two years in the group?

- How helpful are the MDs and VPs when analysts complete their analyst programs? Will they help analysts with recommendations to outside options? Business school applications?

What Should I Do if I Get Placed into a Bad Department?
This is usually a difficult situation. Most likely, either you didn't do so well during the summer training program, or something happened behind the scenes when the departments were negotiating who they wanted. No matter how disappointed you may be, the most important thing to do is to make the most of it and keep a positive attitude. Unfortunately, typically with most analysts who are in this situation, they take it for granted and forget how hard it was to get to that analyst position in the first place. If you work hard, do a good job and show a positive attitude, the people you work for will likely be more accommodating in helping you out with getting you a chance to rotate to an area that you prefer later on. Without support from your own group (HR will ask your managers about your performance), no other departments will consider you, that's as simple as it gets. An alternative strategy is to try and get into a different firm and see if you can get into a better department

there, but if you get discovered, it could ruin your relationship internally and unexpectedly shorten your analyst career.

Every year there will always be one of two groups that are the "hot" groups, which seems to coincide with key cycles in the stock market. M&A is usually one of the hot groups, but when the Internet bubble burst in 2001, that was the least desired group because there was no deal flow; although today it has returned to being one of the favored groups, analysts are weighing lifestyle issues more seriously than they had before and dodge the M&A group like the herpes virus. In some large firms, because of the M&A group's reputation for burning out analysts (high turnover), some trainees are forced into the group because the group needs more bodies.

It's important to keep in mind is that just because a group is not popular does not necessarily mean it's a bad group. The reverse is also true of the popular groups. Analysts sometimes get caught up with drinking the Kool-Aid of the popular groups naively believing all the positive aspects without taking into consideration the negative aspects. One extremely bright analyst in my JP Morgan training program ended up going into an unpopular group called STRAPS, a very esoteric area that specializes in complex structured products that help clients with complicated tax issues; that particular analyst ended up getting promoted early without an MBA and after a couple years of experience, was making nearly triple the amount of money the rest of his peers were with the same years of experience. The opportunity is what you make of it.

Traits of a Star Analyst

What differentiates a star analyst from an average one? Perhaps a better way to ask that question is, what traits are typical of most star analysts. A star analyst works hard, has enthusiasm, is a perfectionist (pays attention to details, so you can be confident of the numbers), and has the initiative to do things without being told. They tend to be efficient and know where to get information, they seem better at knowing how to leverage resources without having to create things from scratch. The star analyst doesn't just crunch numbers but understands why the numbers are what they are, and asks good questions. Ultimately, the analyst becomes the one that most associates hope to get staffed on their projects.

Analyst Staffing

Sometimes working on one major transaction early on will make you known by the rest of the group and catapult you forward. If you are in a large department where there are 10-15 other analysts, and the deal flow isn't as good, the analyst that gets staffed on a live deal early on will most likely have the best opportunity to become the star analyst. This is why having a good relationship with the staffer is so important because he/she can ultimately determine the future of your analyst career based on the projects you get staffed on.

Good staffers will allocate projects fairly as they new projects arise, spreading live deals across all the analysts. Unfortunately, this isn't always the case as there is usually significant politics and jockeying involved. Sometimes senior members of the team will put pressure on the staffer for certain analysts that they prefer (the star analyst) and if you aren't that person, the rest of your analyst careers could be focused on doing pitches rather than live deals. Thus, if you don't have a good relationship with your staffer, the best thing to do is try to be chummy with some of the senior folks that you seem to like or have good reputations; they may ask for you to be staffed on their projects.

VI. Questions You're Afraid to Ask But Wish You Could

We've all been there, those awkward situations where you don't know what to do.   This is a list of some potential events/situations that may arise and ways to handle them.   As silly as some of the situations may seem and basic common sense would tell you the right thing to do, you'd be surprise how many actually don't seem to know what to do in those circumstances; I've seen it happen to a number of analysts.

Resume/CV/Cover Letter
How many pages should a resume be?
I don't care how much experience you think you have, but if you are an undergrad or have only a couple years of work experience after an MBA program, you should limit your resumes to only one page.   You can have a supplemental page that lists deals/transactions that you've worked on before if you are an associate that had prior investment banking experience.   The majority of the time, interviewers will spend five minutes looking at your resume, so you need to make a very quick first impression.   Learn to be concise and get the key points about you across without making the reader dig for it, this is good business writing.   Unless you're a Vice President or Managing Director, I would shy away from two-page resumes.

Should I list all the extra-curricular activities that I am involved with, or just the ones that are significant to me?
Since resumes are meant to be the first impressions that you want a recruiter to have of you, it's very tempting to list lots of extra-curricular activities to show you're an active person outside of school.   The fact is, interviewers aren't stupid, so they

will know if you're just trying to window-dress and it could be more harmful than helpful. You should mainly list the activities where you had significant involvement (i.e., you held a leadership role, or managed a major event sponsored by an organization). It may be okay to list some activities from High School if you're stretched to find things to fill space.

Should I include my GPA / SAT / GMAT scores?

The general rule for GPA is that you should include it if it's above 3.3 but exclude it otherwise. Recruiters make an assumption that it's below a 3.3 if you exclude it. As for SAT and GMAT scores, include it if you did well, but obviously exclude if it's just average (SAT over 1400; GMAT over 700).

How important are cover letters?

Personally, as an interviewer I rarely read cover letters because the resume is the meat of the information that I need to know about the individual. Some do find it useful to introduce things that may not be as apparent on the resume. If you are going to provide a cover letter, you should keep it limited to three short paragraphs. Again, keep it concise and focus the reader on why you are a great candidate with key bullet points similar to a resume.

Eating/Dining Situations

What types of food should you not order during important meetings with clients and team members that you are trying to impress? Or even on sell days?

When you're at a sell-day, a lot of companies will try to wine and dine their potential hires, lavishing them with wine and food by taking them to the best dining places. You should definitely enjoy yourself, but don't get too loose. Be careful because these are also interviews. You are still being judged, and even if you had your written offer already in hand and guaranteed a position with the company that's taking you out, don't be surprised if that offer is rescinded following a bad and embarrassing dining experience. They want to impress you and convince you to join the firm, but they also want to judge you in social settings. Just because you've been given an offer and are being "sold" about the potential employer doesn't mean you have a right to be a total baboon without recourse. Here is a list of some major don'ts:

- Don't get drunk, no matter how wonderful the wine may be and how rare you get to be wined and dined. There are plenty of opportunities to get drunk without as significant a consequence.

- Don't order the most expensive entrée on the menu, just because they're paying for it doesn't mean you should blow their budget. There is really no free lunch or dinner.

- Don't order food that gets too messy. Spaghetti is one prime example. It'll splatter, causing embarrassment on you, and even worse, if you splatter it on your neighbor, make you look like an idiot.

- Don't be a pig. Use your judgment. If you're at a pre-interview dinner (usually the night before the Super Saturday), you'll have other candidates there with you and while you want to stand out in the eye of the potential employer, don't stand out in a bad way. Know your table manners.

I don't know table manners, what should I do?

Not everyone grows up eating with perfect dining etiquette simply because most people are not that particular about it. Nobody cares if you wolf your food down when you're sitting in front of the TV or at a bar with your buddies. However, for business functions, it's better to err on the safe side to know and follow correct table manners. If you don't know which forks to use for which course, the simplest thing to do is watch someone else. I recommend reading the Emily Post Book of Etiquette to familiarize yourself with accepted standards.

If someone else at the table has the wrong dining etiquette, should I correct them?

It's best not to correct them unless they ask you. On this issue, if you try to correct them, you'll seem like a know-it-all, or even worse, a prick.

Do I have to drink at social events?

I have only known one banker who didn't drink. Drinking and business seem to be permanently married. If you love to drink, banking will certainly improve your alcohol tolerance and eventually your waist size. If, on the other hand, you can't hold your alcohol, you're going to be at a bit of a disadvantage because everyone else is drinking. Asians in particular, tend to be susceptible to this dilemma, although that's not to say there aren't any Asians who can drink like a whale. Even though usually people will not directly pressure you to drink, you will feel a bit left out and awkward if you're the only one not drinking.

There are several ways to handle this. One is to order cranberry juice. Why cranberry juice as opposed to orange juice, or coffee, or tea? Well, a number of mixed drinks incorporate cranberry juice, so it's hard to tell if there's no alcohol in it, so it's rather subtle, and only people sitting near you will know if they heard your order.   If you are really pressured into ordering something alcoholic, order a beer or some low-alcohol drinks like pina coladas and strawberry daiquiris. Most places will make virgin (non-alcoholic) versions of those drinks as well. Other common virgin drinks include "virgin mary" or "virgin margarita" that you can specify to the waiter.

There will be times when some team members or clients will order the wine or alcoholic beverage for you, so you won't have the choice of ordering a non-alcoholic version. The best thing to do in that situation is to make sure you also ask for a glass of water. Even though you have the glass of wine in front of you, you don't need to drink the whole thing. When someone is doing a toast, just take a little sip to be considerate and polite, you don't have to gulp down the whole glass. Try to eat something heavy (examples include steak, cheese, etc.), which will reduce the impact of the alcohol.

What you should do when one of your team members have something stuck on their teeth?

First all, this does happen, more frequently than you realize. If you are having dinner or lunch with your team member, and this is purely an event with your own team/company, then you should definitely inform the individual who is unaware of his/her predicament. Usually this is easier to handle when the team members are your peers and not a very senior team member, but regardless, you should always inform them if they have some obtrusive unintended decoration on their tooth. A simple statement like "Bob, I think you have something on your tooth" should be sufficient.

What if it's a client member who has something on his/her tooth?

The same answer applies. Be polite and notify them without making a scene and wait until they stop talking rather than interrupt them in the middle of a sentence to do so. Sometimes, a simple hand signal (index finger pointing at your own teeth) can provide the necessary message.

How do I avoid or reduce the chance of getting something stuck on my own teeth?

The first level of defense is to avoid food that may increase the chance of getting something stuck on your teeth. Examples of this include salad and food that comes in little bits, like peppercorn or parsley. If you happen to eat food like that, then your second line of defense is to learn to swish water in your mouth in an inconspicuous manner when you're done chewing.

Cell Phones and Blackberry

When I was a college student, very few people had cell phones. Today they have become almost universally accepted as a "must have" among college students. There are some cell phone etiquettes that should be adhered to.

What should I do if my phone or pager rings when I'm in the middle of a dinner with a client or team?

Some restaurants prohibit cell phone usage in their dining area. The best way to prevent something like this from happening is to turn your cell phone off or set the ringer to vibrate instead beforehand. If you accidentally forgot, you should quickly find it, turn it off, and apologize when it rings.

What if I have an urgent call that I must take?

Albeit rare, there are times when you really do need to take urgent calls, so the best thing to do is to politely excuse yourself and find an area with privacy; make it short and quick. Apologize for the interruption when you return. Nevertheless, try to let people know in advance when the best time to call so that there are no awkward interruptions.

Regardless, you should always have your cell phone or black berry set to "vibrate" when you are in a meeting, and even just in the office. Should you need to keep it on a ring tone, at least make sure the ring tone isn't something annoying and unprofessional in office settings.

Dress Code

Back in the old days, this was a very simple matter. Everyone on Wall Street had to wear a suit. Whether the weather was 10 degrees outside or 100 degrees, there was just no excuse for not having a suit on. In fact, up until 1999, almost every major Wall Street investment bank still had a formal dress code and required a suit. There was no question of when you had to and when you didn't, it was simply required. A few had casual Fridays over the summers, but even then, it was only one day out of the week. With the bubble years of the Internet lifestyle, which in some ways, resembled the liberalization movement of the hippies in the 1960s and 1970s, a revolution of attitude and dress code slammed Wall Street as younger bankers were being drawn to the technology startups that had no dress codes and a hipper working environment. To compete, some firms started having casual Fridays year round, while others implemented significant loosening of their dress code policies allowing business casual year round and only requiring suits when there were client meetings. With the crash of the technology boom, not surprisingly, some of the firms started to go back to their old dress codes. My best advice would be to dress conservatively, it's always better to err on the conservative than being too loose.

What do I wear to recruiting events?

Every school hosts recruiting events and have recruiters from various employers give presentations. Recruiting starts at this point, so it's best to be prepared. Don't wear anything that you would be embarrassed about later on. Companies will host receptions at schools as a way to advertise themselves there, and most of the time, the representatives there will also be the ones who will have some role in the interviewing process, not to mention the resume selections for prescreening. You want the people to remember you, but in a favorable way. Most likely, if you are casual showing up for the recruiting presentations (which is usually the case for most students), you will be just one of the many students there. This is fine, but if you are serious about getting a job with that company, you should try to stand out in front of the crowd.

You may feel a bit awkward about wearing a suit to the presentation, but if you're one of the few students who show up wearing a suit or a sports jacket, recruiters will remember that and know that you're serious about their firm. If you show up wearing ripped jeans and pink spiked hair, you'll likely be remembered as well, but probably not in the way you want. This might have been okay for an Internet startup company recruiting on campus in 2000, but chances are, even those firms that have survived wouldn't look at someone with that dress code these days.

What should I wear to a dinner hosted by recruiting company?

Sometimes as a way to narrow down the stack of resumes down even further to limit the number of invitees back for final rounds (most often called Super Saturdays), some companies will host dinners at the school where alumni currently at the company are there to help answer questions. It also gives them a chance to woo the more attractive candidates.

If you aren't told or aren't sure of what to wear, you should wear a suit to be safe. You can always take the tie off or jacket off if you arrive and the representatives from the company are all dressed casually. You want to fit in and it's much harder to do so when you're dressed casually while everyone else is in a formal suit.

You should not hesitate to call and ask the person who invited you to the event what the dress code is. Just say you're "calling to confirm that the dress code is suit and tie" and hear what their response is. Even though you might think it's an awkward question, it actually serves a few positive purposes for you. Firstly, it shows the company's recruiters that you're thinking ahead and you are well-prepared. Secondly, it confirms to them that you're serious about getting a job with them to care enough to think about something like that. Thirdly, it'll get your name into their head and they'll be more likely to remember you. Finally, if it turns out that the dress code is casual, you will know ahead of time and can therefore dress accordingly.

Making Contact and the Methods Used

It used to be so simple until technology and the need to be connected started complicating this. Now, cell phones are so prominent and email becomes the most efficient document transfer method that it can be a bit confusing as to what is the appropriate way to contact someone, be it HR, an alumni of your school that is at the firm you are interested in, or even just someone you met at a reception.

Some words of caution on email

Email is truly the most efficient way to communicate, but it also could lead to rather precarious embarrassments as well when imprudently used. Always treat communication related to recruiting formally as if it were a normal business letter. That means no smiley faces, incomplete sentences, slang, etc. Always check and proof read your email before sending it out; the last thing you want is a potential employer to get the impression that you are lackadaisical when there are typos in the message, especially after you've spend weeks revising, scrutinizing and perfecting your resume. Always make sure the name is spelled correctly of the person you are addressing. Misspelling someone's name implies you are (1) careless, (2) disrespectful, and/or (3) not interested in the position enough to make sure you are presenting yourself in the best light.

Should I email my resume or should I submit a hardcopy?

When I was an undergrad, even though email was starting to be more widely used, every company still asked for resumes on hardcopy. Now, I think the choice may be shifting towards email, although I would suggest sending both. You will probably have to drop your resume in hard copy to the Career Services Office at your school that typically collects it and sends it on to the recruiting firms; make sure you do so by the drop date. With the advances in technology, some schools use virtual drop boxes where you just upload the resume instead of submitting a hard copy. You can always email an updated copy of your resume to the appropriate people as a follow up, just don't miss the deadline.

Should I email, or send a regular thank you letter, after an interview or meeting someone from the company?

It is sufficient to send an email. These days, everyone checks emails in the office. I would recommend sending a thank you email no later than two days after the interview or meeting someone that you had talked to about a potential job opportunity. You can also follow up with a phone call as well, although not necessary, unless you felt there was something you had missed in your email.

Is it true that my work email is screened?

Yes. With the level of scrutiny that securities firms face today, all email gets screened through a filtering program for certain words. If you send an email from work to a home email address, it can be traced (former employees have been fired for doing that as most firms now make it a violation of company policy). The same applies to your blackberry since it goes through the same corporate email system. Thus, word from the wise, don't send anything by email that you wouldn't feel comfortable having someone from work reading.

On the Job

Who do I ask for help when I have questions when I first get into a department?

Most analysts tend to be shy about asking questions because they're afraid of appearing stupid. Unfortunately that's also a recipe for disaster. Analysts are not expected to know much when the first join, and therefore should ask lots of questions, you usually have a pretty long grace period where you can ask questions without sounding dumb. The first person to ask if you can't figure something out yourself are the analysts who are just a year ahead of you. They know exactly what you're going through so don't hesitate. If they don't know the answer, then ask the associate. It's probably not a good idea to hop into the MD's office to ask a question unless you have a great repoire with that individual; some firms are less bureaucratic and that may not be an issue, but most of the time it's not the case.

I found a mistake in the presentation and it's about to get sent out, who should I tell?

This happens, and it happens a lot! Most of the time, you'll catch a mistake before the printing process and the presentation hasn't been printed and bound. The best way to handle this is to ask the associate, then you push the ball into his/her court and they will be the ones making the final decision as to what the best way to proceed. If the mistake is minor, most likely they will let it slip. But if is a numerical error that flows into other parts of the presentation, the probability is high that the pages will need to be torn out and replaced.

Can you date someone in your office?

This is not a good idea, although it happens because you spend so much time in the office and have a very limited social life outside of work. Most of the time the outcome is not a good one. If you are going to date someone in your office, at least try to make sure it's not someone in the same department. At Morgan Stanley, there is a subtle policy that forbids spouses to work in the same departments. Rumors spread like wildfire, so it is best to avoid such a situation.

I think my boss is hitting on me, what should I do?

This is one of the very awkward situations. There are situations when an MD hits on a young new analyst and it was okay back in the heydays of Wall Street, but now given significant regulatory scrutiny, firms are extremely careful about their reputations.   If you suspect a situation that makes you uncomfortable, talk to HR.

I'm pretty swamped with five projects, but the staffer wants to put me on another one, how do I handle it?

First of all, it depends on what types of projects you're working on.   If the five projects you are currently staffed on are all pitches, and the new project that the staffer wants to put you on is a live deal, the answer is obvious, take the live deal!   Of course, let the staffer know your capacity so he/she can manage to lower the priority with the managers of your pitch projects, or even pull you out of one of the other pitches.

Unfortunately you usually don't know what the new project is going to be until you've mentioned your capacity to the staffer, but sneaky analysts will usually sniff out in advance through their managers and know a staffing is coming, as well as some insights as to the type of project.   Associates are usually staffed first, then they request an analyst to be staffed, so if you hear the whispers of a new project from the associates, you know some analyst is about to get hit with a staffing.

I'm not getting staffed on good projects, what do I do?

You should talk to the staffer and see what can be done. Sometimes the reason for it is beyond their control (for example there just aren't good deal flow), but other times, it could be something more controllable.   If that still doesn't remedy the situation, and you suspect some bias in the staffing, you can talk to HR or some of the more senior managers in the department who may be able to pull you into a deal if they like you.

Someone sent an email to the group distribution list through my computer as a prank, how do I handle that?

Certain departments are notorious for having mischievous pranksters in the analyst class, sort of a hazing period when senior analysts try to indoctrinate the newer analysts into the group. You need to know what's merely fun and games and what could be potentially damaging when a prank goes too far. If the email sent out fits into the later category, you should send a follow up email notifying others that it wasn't you. It's like high school, you want to be "cool" to your peers in the department, but you also have to know when to draw the line. Sometimes it's not too late to retract the email in outlook, or you can call IT see if they can retract it to limit the number of people the email had been sent to; this usually only works if the recipient hasn't opened up the email. The best defense against something like that is to lock your computer before you walk away from your cube.

A client wants to take me to a strip joint, what do I do?

In the old days, this was a fairly common practice. With significant regulatory scrutiny faced by every firm now, you can be fired for doing something like that. The best response is to just let the client know you are prohibited from participating in such events and let your manager know. That way, if the client insists, you can push the decision to your manager. Fortunately such a predicament will be less common for junior bankers.

I just finished my first year as an analyst, should I stay to complete the second year?

This is a very difficult decision to make and will depend on what your make objectives are. Having investment banking on your resume will help you in opening doors to other options, but having only one year doesn't quite pack a punch. People usually want to see at least two years as an analyst because that shows that you've truly had a real analyst experience. The years go by very fast and you may not get as much exposure and responsibilities until you're a second year analyst. The second year is also an improvement because there is more interesting work and less of the pure grunt work that first year analysts get piled with.

If the reason you want to leave after a year is because you have some great opportunities outside, that's a great situation to be in, but doesn't necessarily mean that leaving is the right option. Chances are, if you are able to get good options outside after a year as an analyst, you will have even better options when you're finishing your second year.

On the other hand, if you're leaving because you haven't had as good an experience during the first year, or you're burned out, then I would suggest you find an option first before you leave. It's much easier to find a new position when you're currently working.

Miscellaneous
Do analysts really work 100+ hour weeks??
Yes and no. Depending on the department, the hours required vary but on the whole, investment banking is a business that requires long hours (excluding sales & trading). Sometimes the work goes through cycles, you could have a 100+ hour week followed by a 70-hour week. Staffers try to be understanding and not staff you immediately after you've just completed a very demanding project, but if the department is short of people, it's going to be a more constant situation. It should be noted that even though you may be in the office for the 100+ hour weeks, you're not constantly working all the time; quite a bit of the time

is spent waiting because you need certain information before other steps in the analysis can be completed, what is often referred to as "down time" and can get pretty frustrating. This is why you are often staffed on multiple projects because you can juggle other things when one project is going through some down time.

Are there still minority or gender considerations in the recruiting process?

HR would not want to admit it but at most large investment banks, there are policies that are intended to improve diversity representation.   Minorities   include   African   Americans, Hispanics, and Native Americans.   Typically the minimum standards required are a bit lower for minorities and women, and a number of interview slots are specifically set aside for them for the initial interview screenings.   This applies to both full time opportunities as well as summer internship opportunities.

I've decided I want to explore other options, how do I proceed?

Usually the options are most available to analysts in their second year.   Using a headhunter is becoming more common place and most efficient because the headhunter serves as the intermediary to help manage the process for you.   There are numerous headhunters out there, but the more reputable ones that focus on analysts include:

- The Oxbridge Group (www.oxbridgegroup.com)

- SG Partners (www.sgpartners.com)

- Glocap (www.glocap.com)

Be careful with using headhunters because some of the less ethical ones may forward your resume when you don't want them to; good ones will ask your permission first before sending it out. The good ones have been in the business a long time and have a strong reputation with their clients that they help recruit for. Some work on a retainer basis (which means that they're hired by an employer such as a private equity fund and paid to find the best candidate that fits what the fund is seeking), while others work on a commission basis (which means that the headhunter will only be paid if a candidate accepts the position…usually about 20-30% of your full package, paid by the employer, not you). Reputable headhunters will typically be hired on a retainer basis by employers.

I have found a position that I want and am ready to quit, who do I tell?

Until you have signed an offer letter, you should always keep things hush hush. If your department finds out you've been interviewing outside, you could be fired on the spot. Obviously not all firms and departments are as selfish but it's always best to be conservative about your assumptions. Goldman, for example, has a reputation for being very helpful to analysts seeking alternative opportunities during their second year, whereas Morgan Stanley is the total opposite and has been known to threaten to call the employer to rescind your offer if they find out who you're looking to join!. Again, these are generalizations, but there is some basis of truth.

The first person you should tell is your staffer. They will make the announcement. If you are close to certain people in the department, out of courtesy, you should tell them directly rather than waiting for the staffer to disseminate the news. The best days to make the announcement is either a Friday or a Monday. Never do it in the middle of the week.

The best way to make the announcement, if the staffer hasn't done so after you've told him/her that you're resigning is to send out a quick short email to your group. Be polite, don't boast, don't get too personal. A headhunter told me once that you shouldn't even send out those farewell emails, but use your judgment. You may or may not want to let people know where you are heading, but you should include a brief statement thanking everyone for the experience you had, and new contact information where you can be reached, if you do decide to send out an email to announce your departure. Just another word of caution, be careful to check the email distribution list…there have been cases where analysts send out a farewell email to a distribution list that was intended just for the group, but given the auto-fill function, accidentally sent it to the whole firm's investment banking division (over 10,000 people) which includes the vice chairman.

Absolutely do not burn bridges, the financial community is a small world. I've heard horror stories of a couple analysts at JP Morgan who were so full of themselves after they had offers to go to a well-known private equity firm that they boasted to the department and offended some people with some of their comments during their exit. The managing director found out where they were going, made a couple calls to his friends at the private equity firm, told the private equity firm about the two, and last I heard, the offers were rescinded. As they say, revenge is sweet. Moral of the story is be careful who you offend because it'll come back to bite you when you least expect it

What happens after you hand in your letter of resignation?

Depending on how your relationship is with the staffer and the group you're working at, the reaction will vary across firms and across departments. Some firms are notorious and ask you to leave immediately, escorting you out without your materials. They will have your assistant pack your cubicle up for you and send it to you rather than letting you do it yourself because they don't want any proprietary information leaving the firm. You'll be asked to leave your blackberry, ID card, cell phone and any other firm-issued items at your desk before you leave. They may check any bags/briefcase you're taking with you to make sure nothing deal-specific or information specific to the firm is taken that does not belong to you. This includes any work (presentations, models, etc.) that you've worked on even if you were the one creating it.

VII. MBA Candidates

Although much of this guide is intended for undergraduates, I'm sure there are some MBA candidates who are also trying to get into investment banking but don't know how to get in. If you're like most MBA candidates from top schools, a Wall Street job is considered the ultimate culmination of your MBA program. Saddled with about $100K+ in student debt, you may not necessarily want to do investment banking long term, but of all career options, this is certainly an area that is one of the highest paying and will be a fast track to paying down all your debt. Fortunately, most top business schools have significant alumni and career services help to prepare you, so don't hesitate to take advantage of them.

Most of the pointers in the rest of the book should be relatively applicable regardless of your status as an MBA candidate or an undergraduate candidate. You are probably more mature and more focused on what you want to do since you already have had good work experience prior to getting into business school. This chapter is a meant to be a short discussion of some areas that MBA candidates may not be aware of, rather than a reiteration of the previous points.

Summer Internships
Like junior year internships for undergraduates, this is an extremely crucial factor for getting a job on Wall Street after you graduate. Most candidates don't realize that internships for Associates typically are given to those that have not had banking experience prior to their business school program. This is both good and bad.

The rationale is twofold. Firstly, analysts that have gotten into business school with previous investment banking experience typically are looking for a career change or at least have other options, so it would not make sense for them to go back to banking for a summer internship again...they already know what it's like. Most are looking to switch to the buyside, whether it's a hedge fund or a private equity firm, where the lifestyle is theoretically better. Secondly, firms prefer to give non-bankers summer associate positions. So if you've been a management consultant, worked in business development, engineer or a marketing person prior to banking, and you are seeking a summer internship in investment banking, the chances are high that you'll get preference over those who already have banking as a background.

As a summer associate, you're paid fairly well, typically prorated to the rate that a full-time hire would be paid. Summer associates are given significant responsibilities and expected to be able to be proficient in financial modeling and accounting, so if you are weak in those areas, make sure you take courses in your first year of the MBA program to prepare rather than waiting until the second year.

Often, summer associates will be receiving guidance from other associates in the group or junior VPs.   A very common situation with most Associates, particularly ones from the top schools, is the fear of asking questions. The reality of the situation is that it would behoove you to ask questions and get the right answers than to guess on a situation and embarrass yourself. If that means asking an analyst for help, do it. The truth is, a third year analyst is way ahead of you because they're in the job that you want to be in; most third year analysts are treated like first year associates because that's how they are expected to perform, so there should be no shame in asking for help from them. Furthermore, third year analysts are not likely going to be the individuals who will review you at the end of the summer.

Differences in Hiring an Associate for Full Time vs. an Analyst

When an investment bank hires an associate, the mentality is very different from hiring an analyst. The explanation can be seen in the relative tenure of the two positions. Analysts are hired with the expectation that they will stay for two years, and invited to stay for a third if they are star performers. The majority of them go back to school or pursue something else after the second year. Associates on the other hand are hired with the hope of being long term bankers at the firm, so the approach is to look for banker potential. This means that cultural fit and a strong desire to work in the industry long term are factors that interviewers will hone in on. Analytical kills and financial modeling skills should be superior since that's what an MBA is supposed to provide as an addition to your prior work experience. For that reason, you can't go into an interview being wishy-washy about the opportunity. Even more important than undergraduate candidates, you really need to convince the interviewer you're the ideal fit with the firm and are looking at the opportunity as a career and not just as a short term job to pay back your student loan, regardless of your real motives.

Although the lifestyle of an associate should theoretically be better than an analyst's, the reality of most firms is that it will be only marginally better. If you ask any senior banker, most would tell you the hardest period as a banker is as an associate. Analysts are responsible for doing the grunt work, but the associate is just as liable. Most associates are working side by side their analysts, rather than dumping the work and just checking them after it's been completed. The worst part is that if there is a mistake, the associate is the one held responsible. Yes, the analyst may have made the mistake, but it's the associate's responsibility to catch and fix it. As they say in banking shit rolls downhill (trickle down effect) when there's an issue; even though analysts may be at the very bottom of the totem pole, they seem to have a shield deflecting the crap back onto you because of the ignorance defense. As the associate on a project, you don't have that luxury. An analyst may get chewed out, but that's short-lived, and they'll just get staffed on a new project; the associate will not only get chewed out, but also lose credibility among team members and that's a career-damaging situation. Rarely do you get a second chance to make a first impression in banking.

The typical associate will spend a little over three years an associate role before being up for promotion to vice president. However, high stress levels, personal life balance considerations and overall happiness tends to push many out of the position before completing their second year. Some of it may be a function of ulterior motives in the first place (paying back MBA loans) in taking the position, so it's not too surprising. However, it would be naïve to believe that other factors do not attribute significantly to the high attrition.

Let me give you a prime example. Joe, a good friend of mine who is now a vice president at one of the bulge bracket firms, had the classic dilemma that many associates endure when deciding between career and personal life. He was a second year associate at JP Morgan's Media & Telecom group at the time when one vice president he was working for kept postponing his vacation on several occasions. Like most associates, Joe bit his lip and pushed on. While last minute changes to vacation plans are common and expected for most bankers, the one event that really crossed the limit for Joe was when his wife had their first baby. He was planning a long weekend trip to Boston with his wife to visit his father and introduce the baby boy to his dad for the first time. Of course, the vice president he was working for didn't even take that thought into consideration and forced him to cancel the trip. Joe took the trip regardless and the next thing you know, the vice president spoke to the head of the group and Joe was out.

While this scenario may sound extreme, it is not an uncommon situation. It was only after a three year period away from Wall Street that Joe returned to investment banking, although he now focuses on a different part of investment banking where the lifestyle is more reasonable.

Moral of the story is that investment banking as an associate and up is synonymous with sacrifice. There is a price to pay and it's usually paid early on in the banking career, starting with the associate level.

Because associates are hired with the expectation that they will be at the firm for a long time, namely to become future managing directors in the firm, the objective is to train them and develop them into that role. The initial training resembles that of the analyst training in the summer, but usually much shorter. Fundamental analytics training is something you should have received in business school, so most of the training focuses on financial products and overview of the firm. As with analysts' training in the summer, networking and bonding with your classmates are key components of the summer training. Most analysts that were directly promoted to associates will also be in the summer training with you.

Once the summer training is over, you then go through several short rotations, usually three rotations, each about two months long. At the end of the three rotations, you are expected to have a "home" with one of the three groups you rotated through. While HR will try to accommodate your preferences in terms of the group that you want to end up in, much of it is a function of the group's demand. You may love one group that you rotated through, but if they don't have the mutual feeling about you, chances are you won't end up there. And if none of the groups that you rotated through picked you to be in their groups, you may get "stuffed" into groups that no one wants to be in, or worse, get booted. Although you are hired with the expectation of being a long term employee, there is no reason why they can't let you go. Wall Street can be heartless when you look at situations like that, but at the end of the day, that's how people are weeded out, justifiably or not. On the positive side, just because you sign on to join a firm does not obligate you to stay with them; like professional athletes, you are a free agent to go as you please when another option may be more attractive.

Appendix A: Reading List

This list includes the reading materials that I have personally found to be helpful. While I could have provided a much more extensive list of materials, that is not the intent. The listed materials below have been included because they have been the most helpful in understanding Wall Street.

- The Wall Street Journal – While this is an expensive periodical to subscribe to ($275 annual subscription), I highly recommend you start reading it to get accustomed to some of the events and news that affects the financial markets. Students typically can get a significant discount for subscriptions, and you can also subscribe to the online version for even less. However, if you were cheap like me when I was a student, you can simply go to the university library's periodical section and read the copy there. Learn to scan the front page for the major points and events that had taken place without having to go through all the articles. Always make sure you become familiar with the major news on the front page. For those who are wired most of the time, an alternative is to subscribe to the online version which is about $89.

- Stocks Bonds Futures Options by The New York Institute of Finance – This book is perfect for anyone wanting to get more information about the financial markets, various financial instruments, and the interconnection of relevant participants in the markets. It's easy enough for newcomers to digest, but also a good non-technical reference guide on my desk.

- <u>Market Wizards: Interviews with Top Traders</u> by Jack Schwager – If you are interested in the Capital Markets side of Wall Street, you should definitely read this.

- <u>The Big Deal</u> by Bruce Wasserstein—Written by a Wall Street veteran, the book provides a good overview and historical perspective of the changing deal environment. I recommend reading this if you want a more detailed perspective of how deals have changed over time.

- <u>The House of Morgan: An American Banking Dynasty and the Rise of Modern Finance</u> by Ron Chernow – Although the book is written about J.P. Morgan, it also gives an excellent historical perspective on how Wall Street has evolved over time.

- <u>Monkey Business</u> by John Rolfe and Peter Troob – Written by two junior investment bankers who talk about their experience at DLJ (now part of CSFB) after graduating from business school, this book provides an amusing, albeit biased, perspective on the investment banking associate's experience. Don't admit to a recruiter that you've read this book!

- <u>Liar's Poker</u> by Michael Lewis – This is the classic book about the trading environment back in the 1980s, from the perspective of a junior trader at one of Wall Street's premier bond trading houses at the time (Salomon Brothers, now part of Citigroup). Don't admit to a recruiter that you've read this book either.

- <u>Keys to Success: The 17 Principles of Personal Achievement</u> by Napoleon Hill –   The principles may not seem like rocket science, but most of the successful people I've encountered tend to possess many of the characteristics mentioned.

- <u>Dictionary of Finance and Investment Terms</u> by John Downes and Jordan Elliot Goodman – A very good little reference to have on your desk.

- <u>Emily Post Book of Etiquette</u> – This book is a well recognized guide for etiquette and should provide enough standards of protocol for business dining events.

Appendix B: Terms and Phrases

While the list below is far from being a complete list of financial terms, it's helpful to understand some of the catch phrases that are often used.   This is not meant to be a financial reference/dictionary but rather terms that are useful to be familiar with when interviewers use them.

- Bank Facility – This is a general term for loans (as opposed to bonds) that a company has in its capital structure. Most companies will have both a term loan or a revolving credit facility ("revolver", which is essentially like have a credit card or line of credit where the company can draw on and pay back whenever it wants).

- Boondoggle – While most trips that you take for business are usually boring and stressful, such as a pitch presentation to a client, a boondoggle is just the opposite.   Usually meant for entertainment and networking rather than actually having a specific business agenda to get done.   Sample boondoggles include closing dinner retreats after a major deal has closed and department retreats.

- Boutique Investment Bank – As the term implies, a boutique investment bank refers to smaller investment banks and advisory firms that typically have specializations in a particular product or industry focus. Most small investment banking firms are referred to as boutiques.

- <u>Bridge Loan</u> – Refers to a short term loan that "bridges" to another transaction, whether that is an asset sale or some other securities issues that takes outs the bridge loan. Usually companies take on bridge loans because market conditions are not optimal for other transactions (for example, the company needs money and wants to issue stocks, but because its stock price has dropped dramatically in the near term, but the company anticipates it's just a short term situation, the bridge loan allows it to get the funds it needs until the stock price returns to levels that make it more feasible to issue stock as it originally planned).

- <u>Bulge Bracket Investment Bank</u> – This term refers to the premier investment banking firms on Wall Street. More specifically, they comprise of Goldman Sachs, Morgan Stanley, Merrill Lynch, JP Morgan, Citigroup (formerly Salomon Smith Barney) and more recently Lehman Brothers.

- <u>Credit</u> – The bank loan department where investment grade bank facilities are originated.

- <u>Confidential Investment Memorandum (CIM or CM)</u> – This is the book that typically is written by the analyst/associate to explain a company and the transaction that is being executed.

- <u>Closing Dinner/Offsite</u> – The extravagant celebratory dinner event that celebrates the closing of a major transaction; key bankers are often invited to participate. On significantly large transactions, closing dinners could span several days in which the client and the key bankers fly off to some resort for fun/golf, in which case it would be called an "offsite."

- <u>CA</u> – Refers to Confidentiality Agreement, where one (or both) party agrees to hold information received confidential.

- <u>Capacity (or Bandwidth)</u> – When a staffer asks you what your capacity or bandwidth is, he/she is wondering how much time do you have to take on another project. Usually analysts dodge bad project staffings like the plague by pretending to have no capacity (e.g., pretending to work diligently when the staffer walks by and complain about how you only had 10 hours of sleep the whole week).

- <u>Commercial Bank</u> – Traditionally, these banks were mainly in the business of making loans and were not allowed to provide advisory services that most investment banks do, and investment banks were not allowed to provide loans; after the repeal of the Glass-Steagall Act (this was the 1933 Act that forced the break up of J.P. Morgan from Morgan Stanley), that prohibition no longer exists and most banks today offer both.

- <u>Data Room</u> – In the past, on M&A transactions, these were rooms where the target company's information files are set up for potential buyers to review. Now, more and more companies set up virtual data rooms by putting the information online into a secure site.

- <u>DCM</u> – Stands for debt capital markets.

- <u>Deal Toy</u> – Usually after a major transaction, bankers will create some form of gift item to commemorate the deal to give to clients and the key bankers on the team; lucites are the traditional items.   They are usually presented at closing dinners.

- <u>Dry Powder</u> – Despite what it implies, the term actually refers to the amount of excess funds a firm has for doing transactions or general operations without having to raise additional funds.   Think of it as the money saved for a rainy day; it's essentially the untapped funds available.   For example, at the time of this writing Microsoft has significant dry powder with approximately $30 billion in cash on its balance sheet.

- <u>ECM</u> – Equity capital markets.

- <u>Fixed Income</u> – Refers to the debt/bond market, instruments that bear an interest payment.

- <u>Fire Drill</u> – A situation that demands emergency attention, meaning something that has to be turned around quickly.

- <u>Fire Power</u> – Usually refers to the capacity a department has for doing the work that needs to get done.   If a department does not have enough fire power, it needs more bodies to get the work done and would likely have to bring in more employees.

- <u>First Call</u> – Has two meanings. It can refer to the centralized third-party data resource provider that some firms subscribe to so they can download published research reports and as other information for a fee. Secondly, it can also refer to the type of relationship that client bankers yearn to have with their clients; if you are a first call relationship with a client, it implies that your relationship with the client is a very strong one and when they have a question or want to do a transaction, you would be the "first call" on their list to make.

- <u>High Yield</u> – Refers to bonds that are rated below investment grade (rated Ba1/BB+ or lower by Moody's/S&P). Also known as junk bonds, they have a higher yield (pay a higher coupon/interest rate) because they are riskier.

- <u>Indentures</u> – Another term for bonds.

- <u>IPO</u> – Initial public offering, the first time a company issues its stock to the market to be traded on an exchange.

- <u>II-Ranking</u> – Institutional Investors' Ranking is an annual survey of the major institutional investors polled by Institutional Investors Magazine to rank research analysts. It is considered the most important ranking where the top-ranked research analysts in their respective categories garner significant prestige and become more highly sought.

- <u>Live Deal</u> – Refers to a transaction that is in process. Typically an idea is pitched to a client by the bankers. Once a client agrees to go ahead and execute the idea, the deal goes "live." As an analyst, these are the deals you want to be working on.

- <u>M&A</u> – Stands for mergers and acquisitions.

- <u>Mandate or Engagement</u> – After hearing the "pitch" presentation, if a client agrees to pursue the idea presented by the banker, the client will "engage" the banker. This is when the transaction becomes a "live" deal rather than just a marketing concept.

- <u>One-Stop Shop</u> – Usually this refers to the major investment banks that try to offer all the products to its key clients (a strategy that the large firms tout as their competitive advantage). Think of a Walmart where you can go for almost all your shopping needs, versus a chocolate store that specializes in only chocolates.

- <u>Pitch Book</u> – The dreaded marketing presentation that most analysts and associates toil into the wee hours to complete. It is usually a presentation to a client for proposing an idea that the banker wants to "pitch" the client to do.

- <u>Road Show</u> – The hectic trip where a client company's management team and the bankers travel to various cities across the country (or internationally if it's a global deal) to meet with institutional investors to pitch its securities and give those investors a chance to ask them questions.

- <u>Staffer</u> – The manager who controls your destiny as an analyst, essentially the person responsible for "staffing" you on projects that arise in the department. They are usually an associate or vice president in the department.

- <u>Super Saturday</u> – The final rounds of interviews, typically held on a Saturday when candidates are brought in from various schools for final evaluation. Typically consists of four to six consecutive interviews. It is now not uncommon to have Super Fridays as well.

- <u>Turn</u> – When a manager asks you to "turn" a presentation, it means he/she wants you to make the edits from the markups on the draft of the presentation that he/she left you.

LaVergne, TN USA
14 July 2010
189439LV00004B/29/A